Other books by Alan Hooker

Alan Hooker's New Approach to Cooking

Vegetarian Gourmet Cookery

Herb Cookery

CALIFORNIA

HERB COOKERY

from the Ranch House Restaurant

BY ALAN HOOKER

ILLUSTRATIONS BY BEATRICE WOOD

EDWIN HOUSE PUBLISHING INC

California Herb Cookery
from the Ranch House Restaurant

By Alan Hooker
Illustrations by Beatrice Wood

Ranch House Restaurant
South Lomita, P.O. Box 458
Ojai, CA 93024
(805) 646-2360

Edited by David Skaggs and Ralph Edsell
With contributions from David Skaggs,
Stuart Farnham, and Christine Denney

Book & cover design/production by
Margaret Dodd, Studio K Communication Arts
Prepress production by Allen Crider

Printed in Hong Kong through
Palace Press International

ISBN 0-9649247-0-6

Library of Congress Catalogue
Card Number 96-83173

Published by
Edwin House Publishing Inc.
P.O. Box 128
Ojai, CA 93024

CONTENTS

Conversation about politics.

Chicken   163

INTRODUCTION

The fun of discovery goes on and on.

The Ranch House Restaurant's reputation has clearly withstood the test of time, as it continues, now in its fifth decade, to provide outstanding California cuisine in a lush, outdoor garden setting.

Accolades for the restaurant began in the early '50s when the late Sheila Graham praised the Ranch House in her nationally-syndicated column, the publicity of which helped to initiate the restaurant's long-standing tradition of attracting celebrities. In the early days there were actors and actresses, such as Tom Ewell, Loretta Young, and Irene Dunne. Since then there has been a procession of famous people: the late John Lennon, and his wife, Yoko Ono, Paul Newman and Joanne Woodward, Marlon Brando, Kirk Douglas, Ann Margret, Robert Redford, and many others.

Through the years articles about the restaurant have appeared in numerous newspapers and magazines, such as the *Los Angeles Times*, *Gourmet*, *California*, and *Travel & Leisure*. Along with praise for the food – the homemade breads and desserts, fresh vegetables, herbs and delicious entrees – the Ranch House wine list, featuring a dazzling array of over 600 imported and domestic wines, has been a consecutive winner of the prestigious Wine Spectator Grand Award since 1985.

The Ranch House Restaurant began its unique evolution in one of the first houses built in the Ojai Valley in 1875, which Alan and Helen Hooker converted into a boarding house in 1949. Both in their late forties, the couple moved to Ojai from Columbus, Ohio, where Alan had spent eight years managing a pie bakery.

The boarders, at first mostly friends, paid $14.00 a week, including meals. Alan did the cooking, which was strictly vegetarian, and Helen had charge of the housekeeping and service at the large table where everyone ate. As the boarders invited guests for dinner, and their guests invited other guests, Alan procured a restaurant license, and in February 1950, the couple christened their vegetarian guest house the Ranch House Restaurant. From 1950 to 1954 they remained up on the hill in the old house serving vegetarian dinners.

In February 1954, the old Ranch House property was sold, and the restaurant closed. It wasn't until roughly two years later that, with the help of a few good friends, Alan was able to build a new restaurant on the half acre of land for sale at the foot of the hill below the old Ranch House. Then, on Thanksgiving Day, 1956, the new Ranch House opened with a maximum seating of sixteen – the price for dinner on opening day, an exorbitant $3.50! A baker was hired, but Alan continued to do all the cooking himself, while Helen again took charge of the dining room as both hostess and waitress. Alan bought secondhand wrought-iron tables from the Oaks Hotel in town; Helen found fifty used chairs on sale at a Mexican restaurant for a dollar apiece; and a friend of theirs, the Ojai artist-ceramist Beatrice Wood, whose drawings are featured in this book, offered to repaint them. A waitress and a dishwasher were hired, and the restaurant opened in time for the Ojai Music Festival, with a new seating capacity of forty people, indoors and outside in the garden.

But even with the restaurant's expansion and generous help from friends, Alan and Helen continued to find themselves struggling to maintain the business, and again the restaurant closed. In order to reopen, two important changes had to be made. First, Alan and Helen decided to save money by living at the restaurant. The original dining room was partitioned off, and part of it was converted into a tiny bedroom with barely enough space for two beds, two small chests of drawers, a little vanity for Helen, and a desk for bookkeeping. A tiny shower was installed, and a door cut through the bedroom wall provided them access to the ladies room. The couple moved in February 1958, and lived there for eleven years, until 1969.

The second major change came with their decision to serve meat. The main reason for the restaurant's closing was that they were still trying to operate as a strictly vegetarian restaurant. Although both longtime vegetarians, Alan and Helen decided to begin serving meat, a decision which helped business significantly.

The Ranch House reopened in February 1958. Now, along with the homemade bread and desserts, and the fresh fruit and vegetables, there were three meat entrees – beef stroganoff, chicken cacciatore, and veal scaloppini – the three most glamorous meat dishes Alan had read about at the time. Alan and Helen were as reluctant about serving wine as they were serving meat. Nevertheless, with the addition of the meat entrees, they decided to allow customers to bring their own wine and pay a corkage fee of 25 cents per bottle.

I wish Alan would come to this table.

(Initially, the brook in the garden served as the only place for customers to chill their white wine!) In 1964 Alan procured a wine and beer license. Knowing nothing about wine, he went down to the corner liquor store, randomly selected six bottles of wine, and typed up a makeshift wine list – a modest beginning for what is considered today one of the best wine lists in the world.

Alan often remarked that he'd had a lifelong love affair with food. Food, its preparation, and the social delight of eating with others were all passions of his. At the age of three, he would stand outside his home in Carpentersville, Illinois, and invite passers-by in for dinner. During the Roaring '20s when he played piano in a jazz band, he'd prepare dinner for the other members of the band while on the road. Constantly experimenting with food, he kept track of all his creations in what he called his "food diaries." Between the years 1958 to 1963, Alan invented hundreds of recipes. From these extensive notes kept over the years came the cookbooks, *Alan Hooker's New Approach to Cooking*, self-published in 1963, and then *Vegetarian Gourmet Cookery* and *Herb Cookery*, published respectively in 1970 and 1971 by 101 Productions. Although *Vegetarian Gourmet Cookery* is in its third printing, the other two books are now out of print.

This present book represents a compilation of the best recipes from *New Approach to Cooking*, *Herb Cookery*, and many unpublished recipes which Alan, David Skaggs and his cooking staff created over the years.

In the introduction to his first book, *New Approach to Cooking*, Alan wrote:

> *If what I am doing isn't fun, I don't want to do it. This goes for cooking: when it ceases to amuse me, I want to quit. When old recipes bore me, I want to create or invent something new. It is in the process of discovering something new that the fun comes, not in what is discovered. Long ago I found that many of the products of such a way of life are soon forgotten, but the fun of discovery goes on and on.*

Although these words are testimony to Alan's creativity and artistry as a cook, having been close friends with him for almost twenty years, until his death in 1993 (just shy of his 91st birthday), I can affirm that he never grew tired of the joy of discovery – be it new recipes, meeting new people, or learning something new about himself.

Alan's spirit lives on in the products of his unique life – primarily the restaurant, which is still as popular as ever, and now this cookbook, filled with delicious recipes.

So, in the words of the master, "You asked for some recipes – well, here they are. Now dear reader, go into the kitchen and see what you can do. Have fun!"

Ralph Edsell
Ojai, 1996

HERBS & SPICES

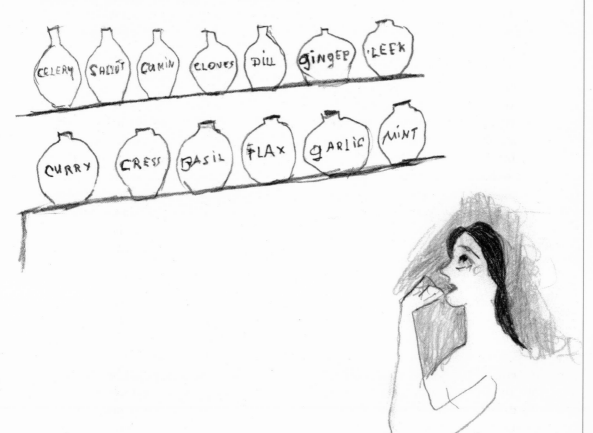

Which should I use?

Growing Your Own

The best place to grow herbs is in a small garden close to the kitchen. Human nature being what it is, when you have to run around the corner of the house for fresh herbs, you'll probably just reach for the bottle on the shelf containing dried ones. So, if possible, arrange it so you can reach out the kitchen door and pluck the sprigs you need. A 3 by 3-foot area will be enough room.

The flavor in herbs and spices is contained in their essential oils. These are developed when the plant has to protect itself from excessive evaporation of its moisture through the leaves. It manufactures oil in the leaves for this purpose, and this oil has flavor.

When I had been in California just long enough to learn to identify its trees, I was driving up the coast along the Big Sur and discovered some bay trees with the longest leaves I had ever seen. I got out and picked some of them and took them home. Imagine my surprise when the leaf I put in the soup disintegrated, leaving only some little sharp pieces that stuck in the throat. On a walk into one of the canyons around Ojai, I again found bay trees, but in this dry area the leaves were thick and tough and very fragrant. They had developed a tough hide and filled it with oil to stop the evaporation of their juices.

I was driving up the coast along the Big Sur.

Storage of Herbs & Spices

So it is with all herb plants. Select a good sunny place where the soil is not too rich. Plant your herbs with room to grow and don't water them too much, only enough to make them grow. A few herbs will need good soil, but let all of them struggle and make more oil for their survival. There is an exception, of course. Parsley needs good soil and plenty of water, but its flavor is strong enough without any struggle to develop it.

If you are an apartment dweller, you can still have an herb garden if you have a window where there is plenty of sun. Herb cooking has become popular, and practically any nursery or even your supermarket will have window–box kits and every kind of aid to start you off.

I repeat because it is so important: the flavor in herbs and spices is in their oils. These oils will evaporate, leaving you with only tasteless, stale or bitter husks. Time, light and heat are the agents that act to deplete these precious oils. Use up your herbs and spices; don't keep them around too long. Store them in tightly stoppered bottles away from sunlight and heat. How many times have you seen an attractively decorated kitchen, with a spice shelf hanging over the stove, or near it, as part of the decor?

Science keeps discovering more curative properties and nutrients in herbs. With the judicious use of them in cooking, one gets all this and wonderful flavor too. So it is worthwhile to give them good care.

Herb Blends

When you have made your herb garden, you will want to blend the ones you dry. Here are suggestions — you may want to change or add to them. Certain foods, however, almost demand certain herbs, such as:

pork — sage; tomato or cheese — basil; fish — fennel; lamb — rosemary.

The following mixtures are given in proportions so that they can be made up ahead of time and stored.

For Soups
2 parts each: thyme or summer savory, parsley, chervil, basil, sweet marjoram
1 part each: sage, rosemary, dried ground lemon peel

For Salads
4 parts each: marjoram, basil, tarragon, parsley, chervil, chives
1 part each: lemon thyme, summer savory

For Vegetables
1 part each: marjoram, basil, celery, parsley, chives
Pinch of: savory, thyme

For Eggs
3 parts: parsley
1 part each: chervil, oregano, tarragon, basil, chives

For Fish
1 part each: tarragon, basil, marjoram, chervil, parsley

For Chicken & Veal
4 parts each: marjoram, basil, chervil, parsley
1 part each: thyme, lemon verbena

For Beef
1 part each: marjoram, basil, parsley, lovage or celery leaves
Large pinch: summer savory, thyme

Savory Herbs
1 part each: basil, oregano, celery tops, parsley, costmary, tarragon
Pinch of: savory, thyme

For Lamb
4 parts each: marjoram, basil, parsley
1 part each: rosemary, savory

Bouquet Garni

For Pork
1 part each: pineapple sage (*or regular sage*), basil, marjoram, summer savory

For Poultry Stuffing
1 part each: marjoram, sage, basil, parsley, savory, celery leaves, dried ground lemon peel

For Tomatoes
1 part: summer savory
4 parts each: thyme, parsley, marjoram, basil

Note: All of the above herb blends are referred to in the recipes — for example, meat herb blend, soup herb blend, fish herb blend, and so on.

When using fresh herbs, you may want to make a bouquet of the sprigs and tie them together with a string or in a cheesecloth bag so that they can be removed when the food is cooked.

A basic bouquet is:
2 sprigs parsley
1 sprig marjoram
1 sprig basil
1 sprig thyme

There are innumerable variations. You could add 1 sprig of any of these:
tarragon, **summer savory**, **dill**, **costmary**, **pineapple sage** (*or a sprig of each of 2 or more*). Put a bouquet in your next pot of soup.

A nice suggestion: Take to a sick friend a little bouquet of fresh, fragrant herbs. It will lift the ailing spirit and help to clear the air.

We should grow herbs for ourselves.

Herb Salt

Blend your own! Start with:
1 teaspoon garlic salt
2 teaspoons onion salt
1/2 teaspoon dry parsley

Next time, add to the above:
1/8 teaspoon basil
1/8 teaspoon marjoram
1/4 teaspoon celery salt

These two herbs are mild.
You might like to add:
thyme or mint, a small pinch
   (careful, don't overdo it!)

This way you will soon learn
the strength of each herb and see
for yourself what you like and
how much of it to use. It can be
great fun.

To release the flavors of the herbs
you are going to add to a dish, grind
them in a mortar with the salt or
herb salt. This blends them before
they go into the mixture. You can do
this with dry or fresh herbs.

*Blend your herbs
but don't overdo it.*

Sesame Salt

Put into a frying pan and heat
gently until the seeds begin
to brown *(do not overheat)*:
8 parts raw sesame seeds
1 part sea salt *(available at
   health food stores)*

Remove and allow to cool, then
put into the blender a little at a time
and run until well mixed. It is not
supposed to be completely smooth;
many of the seeds should still be
whole. Sprinkle this on foods at the
table – soups, salads, entrees – but
when you do this, don't use too
much salt in cooking. This mixture
gives wonderful texture and flavor.

Dessert Spice Blend

The traditional spices most widely used are cinnamon, nutmeg, cloves, allspice and ginger, in the order given. You can put them all together in a blend that does not have one overbalancing flavor!

2 teaspoons powdered cinnamon
2 teaspoons ground nutmeg
1 teaspoon powdered ginger
1/2 teaspoon powdered allspice
1/4 teaspoon powdered cloves

Mix them ahead of time and use the mixture in spice cakes, cookies and pies with delightful results.

For extra–special pastry concoctions, you can enlarge on this by adding a few of the more unusual spices such as:
1/2 teaspoon mace
1/2 teaspoon ground coriander
1/2 teaspoon ground cardamom

Far Eastern Spice Blends

If you use other spices, beyond those in the last recipe, you will be going in the direction of the exotic East. Thus for Western tastes proceed with caution, but proceed!

One of the foundations of good curry powder is **turmeric**. Flavor is then added with **coriander**, **cardamom**, **ginger** and **fenugreek**. Now comes the hot part: **cumin** with its slightly bitter taste and good pepper hotness; **chilies** of many types, fresh or dried, green or red, large and small; and **black peppercorns**.

Pan–cooked vegetables give you a good chance to try out spice combinations. Always use small amounts of spices to get the sense of their individual flavors. You must educate yourself. No one can teach you about flavors; your own palate will tell you all you need to know. Trust it and it will serve you well all of your cooking life.

Curry Powder

In India, it is said that there are as many varieties of curry powder as there are cooks. Since anyone who is interested in using herbs and spices in cooking will want to have at hand a good curry powder, here is a chance to be creative. Start off with a good but simple blend.

Grind in the blender or with mortar and pestle until powdery fine:

6 tablespoons coriander seed
1/8 teaspoon cayenne pepper
1 1/2 tablespoons powdered turmeric
1/2 tablespoon whole cloves
1 1/2 tablespoons fenugreek seed
1/2 tablespoon cardamom seed
1 1/2 tablespoons cumin seed

If you don't have a blender, using the mortar and pestle will make a lot of work – but be sure and pound the mixture well until it is a fine powder.

He uses herbs from India.

The Various
Herbs & Spices

Many authorities classify herbs as the soft part of plants — their leaves and blossoms; spices the hard part — the seeds, bark, roots and kernels. Usually herbs are mild, spices are stronger. Experienced cooks may use a mixture of the two, but caution is necessary because the wrong combination can produce a small tragedy.

Allspice. This is so named because it combines the flavor of cinnamon, cloves and nutmeg, and hints of more. It is the dried and unripe fruit of the evergreen pimenta tree that grows in Jamaica. Its subtle taste is found along with other flavorings in chutneys, pickles and ketchup. It combines happily even in sausage and poultry blends, and fruit cake or mince pie simply would not be what they are without it.

Angelica. Garden angelica, or "the herb of the angels," was so named because it was supposed to have dispelled the plague and protected from harm all those who used its leaves. In France, it is candied and used for flavoring, as well as in many liqueurs such as anisette and Benedictine. All parts of the herb are aromatic; the leaves are especially good in fish dishes.

Anise. This is one of the oldest known herbs and was even praised by Pythagoras. The tops are very good in cooking if used sparingly. The licorice-flavored seeds, known as aniseed, may be used in pastries, soups and teas, and as a flavoring for candies and liqueurs. Mixed with lard, anise is said to relieve itching from insect bites.

Balm Lemon. These very hardy, intensely fragrant leaves are inclined to be bitter in cooking, but are very useful combined with other herbs, such as borage, marjoram, thyme or basil.

Basil, Sweet. There are probably some sixty species of basil differing in height, color and taste, and it is one of the most widely used herbs known. The sweet and purple varieties are very common and essential in Italian cooking. Sweet basil has the capacity of sweetening foods like tomatoes. It is also used in vinegars, soups, salads (*fresh*), cottage cheese, egg dishes, meats, fish and chicken.

Bay Leaf. Bay leaves may be used in all meat cooking, soups, vegetable cocktails, and always in pickle spices. When boiling shrimp, it is essential to put bay leaves in the water; they impart a subtle flavor which diminishes the fishy taste. In Europe the leaves are from the bay laurel tree; the California bay tree is a different variety. The ancient Greeks wove the bay laurel leaves into a wreath to crown their victorious warriors, thus the word "laurel."

Borage. This plant produces beautiful blue flowers all summer. Its leaves are useful in fish, soups and salad dressing.

Burnet. This herb has the flavor of cucumber so that those who cannot eat cucumbers can use this instead. Its leaves are delightful in salads or iced drinks.

Capers. These plants grow wild along the mountainsides in Africa, Italy, France and Spain. The flower buds are gathered early in the morning before they open, and are pickled in vinegar and brine. Capers are a delicious addition to sauces, especially beef gravy, and to salads and canapés. They are used extensively in fish sauces.

Caraway. The seeds of this plant have many culinary uses. They are often used in cookies and breads, especially rye, and will add zest to cheeses, German sauerkraut, and soups like clam chowder.

Cayenne & Chilies. These are the hot red varieties of the enormous pepper family, the fruit of the tropical capsicum plant. There are said to be over 100 varieties of peppers, varying in size and flavor according to their species. The two most common types of chili pepper are the small Japanese chili which is extremely hot and should be used sparingly, and the larger Mexican chili which is much milder. Cayenne is the ground–up version of the red pepper, and is an excellent addition to sauces, omelets and ragouts.

Celery. In America we are not inclined to think of celery as an herb because it is so commonly served as a raw appetizer, especially in restaurants. The seeds, salt and dried leaves, however, are used as a flavor ingredient quite extensively. Cut off the tops of celery, wash and dry the leaves, and then store them in a brown paper bag for use in seasoning soups and sauces. In the wild, celery is extremely bitter; even after cultivation it is considered a bitter herb and thus blends best with the bitter fowls like chicken and turkey, especially in stuffings and soup.

Chervil. This is used in all the French fines herbes blends and in the bouquet garni. Because its flavor is similar to celery, the two may be interchanged in recipes. Chopped fresh, it is excellent in tossed green salad, sauces like Béarnaise or in butter sauce for chicken. Medicinally it has been used on bruises. In ages past, a drink made of ground chervil and wine was supposed to soothe the lungs.

Chicory. The roots are ground up and roasted to add a bitter taste to coffee such as is found in New Orleans. The leaves are the slightly bitter chicory lettuce used in salads. Propagation is by seed.

Chives. The chopped leaves impart a mild onion flavor to soups, cheese omelets, fish and salads, making it essential to any kitchen garden.

Cilantro. This parsley–like plant, grown from coriander seeds, is often called Spanish parsley, Chinese parsley, Hungarian parsley, and so on, depending on the country where it is grown. (*To add to the confusion, "Italian" parsley is a different variety altogether.*) You should know how it looks, smells and tastes so that you can recognize it. Cilantro is short–stemmed with thin, round, lightly fringed leaves. Both the smell and taste are quite pungent. Cilantro is easy to grow. Just get a package of coriander seeds from the grocery and plant them in a sunny location. Water generously and soon the little green shoots will appear. Cut the plant back after it has started branching and it will then send out more shoots. The leaves can be chopped and frozen in a sealed container. This way you will always have fresh cilantro; the frozen plant is just as good as the freshly picked. It does not dry well at all because it loses its color and most of its fragrance. If you let it flower it will go to seed, which can be dried and stored as coriander.

Cinnamon. Even the sound of the name of this most used spice is exotic. The best flavored cinnamon comes from Vietnam, from the ground–up bark of the evergreen cassia trees. When the tree matures the bark is stripped from it, and the tree then dies. After each harvesting, new trees are planted and this cycle of harvesting and planting is maintained by the ceremonial planting of new trees on all festive occasions. True cinnamon (*not the cassia variety*) is light brown in color, almost yellow, and much more delicate in flavor. Practically all of the cinnamon used in America is the stronger flavored cassia.

Cloves. These are the unopened flower buds of one of the most beautiful of the evergreen trees, another of the cassia species. The Dutch name is *kruidnagel*, literally herb nail or spice nail; and the French call them *clou*, from the Latin *clavus* – nail. Cloves are used regularly in canning, pickling, baking and so on because they bring such zest to the flavoring.

Coriander. The ground seeds are used in making curry powder and to flavor pastries, cheeses, vinegars and some sausages. A whole seed, freshly crushed, gives a cup of coffee an interesting flavor. English and Scotch candies were flavored with it years ago. The leaves are similar to parsley (*see Cilantro*).

Costmary. The leaves, steeped fresh, are used mostly as a tea, supposed to have curative powers as a tonic and nervine. This mild, sweet herb imparts a slight flavor of mint, and is especially good in soups, sauces, chicken and fish dishes.

Cress (Overland Cress). Grown on land, this has a flavor similar to, but stronger than, watercress. It may be used in salads, soups, sauces and with chicken and fish, as well as in herb butters.

Cumin. In India, I am told, the whole seeds are used extensively in rice and curry dishes. In America, they are usually ground into a powder. Cumin is a basic ingredient of all prepared chili and curry powders. Its hotness and bitterness make its presence known whenever used, so add it with caution. It can be blended sparingly with many soft cheeses, and spaghetti sauce almost demands a touch of cumin.

Dill. Chopped dill leaves are a flavorful addition to fish, egg and cheese dishes, and to salads. The seeds are commonly used in pickling spices, as well as in apple pie, pastries, spiced beets, some soups, cabbage and sauerkraut. The Greeks believed dill to be so nourishing that athletes were required to eat it in all their food.

Fennel. The ancients said that snakes, which are especially fond of fennel, are made young again by this herb. In Europe the root is cooked as a vegetable. It may also be sliced raw in salads, grated into fish dishes, or brewed as a mild tea. Fennel tastes like anise, but its flavor is weaker.

Fenugreek. The seeds of this Eurasian plant are used primarily for making curry powder. It also makes an excellent tea which some say relieves nausea.

Flag (Sweet Flag). The roots are cut up and boiled in a syrup to flavor confections, custards and puddings. It is also used in cough syrup.

Flax. The uses for flax are more medicinal than culinary. Boiled with grapefruit it makes a drink which relieves colds. A mild laxative may be made by boiling the seeds in water, until a thick liquid is produced. To make a hot poultice, prepare a thick paste with the seeds and water and spread it on flannel.

Garlic. Need anyone ask about its use in cooking? Garlic is also purported to have many medicinal uses and, in the garden, is an insect repellent.

Geranium. There are some 75 varieties of fragrant leaf geraniums – apple, camphor, lemon, nutmeg, orange, almond, peppermint, licorice, rose, and others. These leaves give a wonderful fragrance to food, but they should be used with care and caution because they are sometimes very pungent. To make an unusual salad dressing in the blender, add them sparingly; they may also be used in poultry stuffing. When making jelly, put one leaf in the bottom of the jar before filling it.

Ginger. Ginger root seems to have been used in cooking throughout all recorded time. It is native to tropical Asia and is available as a dry spice, used almost as much as cloves. Who is not familiar with ginger bread and ginger ale? Fresh ginger root is becoming more readily available in American markets. Grated, it is an exotic addition to salad dressings, many meat and chicken dishes, and almost all Oriental cooking. The best ginger comes from Jamaica; it is also grown in Africa, India, and the West Indies. The Chinese and Japanese roots are usually preserved for shipment here.

Horseradish. What would the English do without this to serve with their beef? It is also excellent mixed with mayonnaise. The root is ground and preserved in vinegar to prepare horseradish sauce. Always use white vinegar to keep the color white; cider vinegar will darken it.

Lavender. The seeds are used for cosmetics and perfumes. Place sprigs in linens to give them a wonderful aroma.

Leek. This is the sweetest member of the onion family. It can be steamed or braised and served as a vegetable, or cooked in soup (*indispensable in Vichyssoise*).

Lovage. The plant looks like celery and has something of the same flavor. Thus in recipes calling for lovage, celery may be substituted. An excellent tea is made from the leaves. Propagation is by seed or by root division.

Mace. This is the outer shell of the nutmeg kernel which has been ground and dried. It is stronger, however, than nutmeg. Mace is usually used in combination with other spices, but it is very good by itself when used to flavor cakes and cookies, as well as sweet vegetables like carrots and new cabbage. Whipped cream and chocolate dishes are enhanced by its addition.

Marigold (Pot Marigold, Calendula). The flowers of this plant have been used since the 15th century in France and England to flavor and color drinks. They may be added to soups, sparingly, used to color cheese, or in place of saffron.

Marjoram, Sweet. This, as well as basil, is one of the most useful sweet herbs. It can be used in all types of cooking, except desserts. Long ago it was used as a tea for nervous headaches.

Mint. The ancients believed that mint aroused latent passions and thus prohibited its use by military leaders, whom they wanted chaste. There are many varieties of mint – apple mint, corn mint, curly mint, variegated pineapple mint, caraway–scented mint, orange bergamot mint, white peppermint, black peppermint, nutmeg–scented mint, water mint, and many others. It is very useful used sparingly with chicken or pork. An infusion makes wonderful tea, hot or cold. Mint sauce is made by boiling the leaves in a heavy sugar syrup and then discarding them.

Mustard Seeds. These are used in all pickling spices and in making curry powder. In India, the black seeds are also used in cooking many different vegetables. We all know mustard sauce as an embellishment to the hamburger and other varieties of beef. But it is also a delicious addition to many cheese dishes, especially cheese sandwiches. There are two varieties of mustard, the black and the white. Mustard leaves steamed with other greens are a delicious vegetable.

Nasturtium. This plant is primarily grown for its beautiful flowers, but the leaves and stems are excellent in salads, and the half–ripened seeds in pickles. Young nasturtium seeds may also be substituted for capers.

Grown for its beautiful flowers.

Nutmeg. This seed comes from an evergreen tree native to the Molucca Islands, although it is now grown in many other neighboring locales. The seed is dried and ground before using. Because the fragrant, pungent oil is volatile, it should be freshly grated whenever possible. Being not so strong as its close cousin, mace, it can be used more liberally in fruitcakes, pies and rolls. Nutmeg also enhances many cream sauces and soups, if used sparingly. It is especially good in custards and eggnogs.

Onion. This bulb is unquestionably the most universal source of flavoring, a basic element in the cuisine of almost every country. Botanists, however, have never been able to establish its original home. Many cooks consider the large, flat white onion to be the strongest flavored of the cooking onions, with the yellow, red, and Spanish, or Bermuda, onion less strong, in that order. The small white onions that are boiled and usually creamed are the mildest. The green onion has a variant that is a multiplier. It is very useful for it can be pulled like garlic and each segment planted to make more plants. Because of the penetrating power of the essence, onions are a wonderful catalyst in cooking.

Oregano (Wild Marjoram). There are many varieties of marjoram, but oregano is used more than any other in Italian, Spanish, Mexican and Greek cooking. Because oregano is very similar to but much stronger than marjoram, the two are never used together. Although oregano may be substituted for marjoram if a stronger flavor is desired, the two are not always interchangeable. For example, when a deeper flavor is desired, as in tomato sauces, oregano is indispensable. In salads, oregano should be used very sparingly; sweet marjoram is preferable. The ancients believed that a drink made with ground oregano and white wine counteracted the poisons from snake and insect bites.

Paprika. In Hungary long ago a queen fell ill. Nothing helped her until a doctor prescribed paprika and she recovered. Hailed as a magic herb, it set off the Hungarian cooking spree that gave us all those delicious paprikash dishes, especially chicken. Paprika has been in good favor with cooks for centuries, and now modern science tells us it contains valuable vitamins and minerals. It is nice to know that this elegant red powder we have been cooking with and using as an attractive garnish is also very good nutritionally.

Parsley. Because of the near fetish of using parsley as a garnish, we sometimes forget its most important values as a flavoring agent and a source of nutrition. Its acid-sweet pungency is a basic flavor in every bouquet garni. Nutritionists say that it has an amazing array of the amino acids that comprise the protein molecule. Thus it deserves a better culinary status than resting briefly on a plate of food and then being discarded. Parsley is not only a seasoning; it can be used as a primary food ingredient, in soup, salad, or deep fried in clarified butter.

Pennyroyal. This herb makes an excellent tea with a mint flavor. For centuries it has been credited with repelling fleas when tied around a pet's neck.

Pepper (Black & White). Both come from the same peppercorns; only the black contains the whole corn. The more delicately flavored white pepper is used in sauces mainly because the black flecks would not be attractive in the sauce.

Poppy Seeds. These are used in baking breads and cakes, and are also an interesting addition to sauces and salad dressing.

Rosemary. This is one of the oldest herbs known and is mentioned in all ancient writings about food. It is an excellent accompaniment to lamb, and can be used sparingly with excellent results in salad dressings, stuffings, herb blends and stews. Rosemary is also used as a moth repellent and, when burned with juniper berries, as a disinfectant.

Rue. In cooking, care must be taken in the amount of this herb used. It may be added sparingly to vegetable cocktails, chicken dishes and stews.

Saffron. The tiny gold-colored stigmas of the *crocus sativus* plant are gathered with great patience in southern Europe and Asia; the Asian variety is darker and better flavored. Seventy-thousand hand-picked blossoms make a pound of true saffron. Now you know why it is so expensive.

Sage. There are many different types of sage, but the most common variety used in cooking is garden sage. Others include pineapple, clary, meadow, black, dwarf and variegated sage. This herb, especially the pineapple variety, blends particularly well with pork dishes, stuffings and sausages. It also combines nicely with soft cheeses.

Savory. There are two distinct types of this herb – summer savory and winter savory. Both are very pungent and strong and should be used sparingly. The summer variety should be used in most recipes calling for savory, such as sauces, egg, fish and meat dishes. Winter savory, which is even more pungent, is the main ingredient used in frankfurters. The ancients claimed that savory mixed with wine prevented drowsiness: it was also said to be an aphrodisiac.

Sesame. The seeds, when roasted, are delicious on top of breads and rolls and added to some sauces. Sesame oil is one of the best and most universally used cooking oils. The dark roasted seeds make a pungent oil used as a seasoning in Chinese cooking. The ground–up raw seeds make a product called tahini.

Sorrel. The tart French variety (*sometimes called Silver Sorrel*) is best for cooking. Garden sorrel is not so well adapted to the kitchen. The culinary virtue of French sorrel, when added to dishes like French onion soup, is that it removes the undesired sweetness without adding a flavor of its own. It is often used in soups and salads for its tartness.

Shallot. This member of the onion family is grown extensively in Europe, but is sometimes difficult to find in America. Its distinctive flavor blends especially well with chicken, and adds great interest to many soups and herb vinegars. It is essential to some sauces like Béarnaise. If you cannot find shallots in your market, onions may be substituted with a pinch of garlic and sugar added.

Sunflower Seeds. The great and beautiful sunflower that Van Gogh painted so magnificently in the south of France provides a pleasant treat with its nourishing seeds. They are available in all health food stores and in many supermarkets. Sunflower seeds çan be used in many ways to add texture and nutrition to foods. They are an excellent addition to breads and loaf cakes. They are also especially good in combination with many vegetables that do not require much cooking; they will become too soft if overcooked. A bowl of the seeds placed on the coffee table is a fine substitute for the candy dish.

Tarragon, French. This herb is indispensable in the kitchen mélange of flavors. Who could imagine Béarnaise sauce without it? I always add a bit of it to scrambled eggs and freshly made mayonnaise. Tarragon is propagated by cuttings or by root division. Some find it difficult to grow; but if you have to buy or beg a large plant each spring, by all means add its enchantment to your cooking habits.

Thyme. Caraway, garden or lemon thyme, what variety do you wish? There is also silver, golden, woody, nutmeg, creeping moss, French and English thyme, as well as many more. The English use thyme along their garden paths, so that when one walks on it, the crushed herb gives off its delightful fragrance. The leaves of lemon thyme are particularly suited to fish, and excellent in many sauces. The English and garden varieties may be used in all beef, lamb, poultry and pork dishes. Thyme is essential to every kitchen because of its ability to enhance combinations of herbs. Along with basil and sweet marjoram, it is basic to almost every herb blend.

Turmeric. This is an East Indian root that belongs to the ginger family. It is flint hard and must be ground to be used. It is not hot but is sharp and has a distinctive aroma, flavor and color.

Verbena, Lemon. This herb should always be used fresh; it loses its flavor when dried. The leaves are often used in fruit drinks, especially in champagne cocktails. To add an unusual flavor to pork or chicken dishes, lay the fresh leaves on top of the meat and bake or steam it in a covered pan. In times past, lemon verbena was used to make fragrant soaps. Its leaves placed between stored bed linen impart a wonderful fragrance. It is best propagated by cuttings.

Woodruff, Sweet. This is one of the sweetest smelling of the perennial herbs. The Germans use it to make their famous May wine, and a sprig of it added to any cheap wine will make it palatable. It also imparts an unusual flavor to fruit punches.

Equivalents

Fresh herbs are always preferable to the dried variety. City dwellers, however, sometimes find it difficult to obtain them. When converting measurements from fresh to dry herbs or the reverse, keep in mind that the dry herbs have had their essential oils concentrated in the drying process. Thus use them in smaller quantity.

A good rule of thumb is:
2 sprigs of any fresh herb
(top 2 inches of the new growth)
equal about 1/8 teaspoon of the dried variety

This will vary slightly according to the age of the dry herb. They tend to lose their bouquet as the months pass, and sometimes a slight bitterness develops with age.

Freshly ground pepper is also preferable. If you do not have a pepper mill, follow this rule:
10 turns of the pepper mill equal approximately 1/4 teaspoon ground pepper

In following the recipes in this book, do not use ground herbs or spices unless specified. They are far more powerful than the whole variety.

Note: Green onion butter, which is called for in several recipes, is simply puréed green and Spanish onions, whipped with salted butter.

SAUCES & CONDIMENTS

Did I misunderstand?

MANY WRITERS HAVE ISSUED REAMS OF MATERIAL, A GOOD PART OF IT GUESSWORK, REGARDING THE DEVELOPMENT OF SAUCES. SOME SAY THEY WERE DEVELOPED TO DISGUISE THE FACT THAT THE FOOD THEY DRESSED WAS NOT ALWAYS FRESH; OTHERS SAY SAUCES WERE INVENTED TO TITILLATE THE JADED PALATES OF THE HIGH AND MIGHTY. MADAME POMPADOUR, ONE READS, BROUGHT FAMOUS CHEFS FROM ITALY TO LEND THEIR MAGIC TO THE CUISINE AT THE FRENCH COURT. WHAT DOES IT MATTER? WHEN YOU COOK, DELICIOUS JUICES DEVELOP IN THE PROCESS, AND ANY IMAGINATIVE COOK IS IMPELLED TO DO SOMETHING TO THEM TO ENHANCE THE DISH. THE GREAT SAUCES CONCOCTED THROUGH THE GENIUS OF CREATIVE CHEFS ARE OUR CULINARY HERITAGE.

A SAUCE SHOULD NEVER OVERPOWER THE FOOD IT DRESSES BUT SHOULD COMPLEMENT ITS FLAVOR, AS A GOOD BÉARNAISE DOES ON PROPERLY COOKED BEEF OR FISH. ANY GRAVY OR LIQUID THAT DEVELOPS IN PREPARING FOOD IS A SAUCE, THICKENED OR FLAVORED WITH OTHER THINGS OR NOT, AND IT SHOULD BE HANDLED CAREFULLY, FOR A POOR SAUCE CAN RUIN GOOD FOOD. FOR EXAMPLE, A PERFECTLY COOKED CHICKEN CAN BE RUINED BY A SAUCE WHICH IS CLOUDY OR LUMPY OR TOO THICK.

A FRENCH PROVERB SAYS: "FRUGALITY IS THE HEART OF GOOD COOKING." NEVER WASTE THE JUICE FROM ANY FOOD. IN COOKING, USE ONLY ENOUGH WATER TO PREVENT BURNING, SO THAT THE LIQUID CAN BE UTILIZED FOR ADDITIONAL FLAVOR. I CANNOT STRESS THIS TOO STRONGLY; ALSO, MUCH OF THE MINERAL CONTENT OF THE FOOD LEACHES OUT WITH THE JUICE, SO FOR HEALTH'S SAKE, CONSERVE IT!

THERE ARE SEVERAL WAYS THAT SAUCES CAN BE THICKENED. A GOOD AGENT TO USE IS A MIXTURE OF TAPIOCA FLOUR AND CORNSTARCH IN EQUAL PROPORTIONS, TO WHICH ENOUGH COLD WATER HAS BEEN ADDED TO MAKE A THIN PASTE. ADD THIS TO THE SAUCE, STIRRING CONSTANTLY, AND THE SAUCE WILL THICKEN. THE VALUE OF THIS COMBINATION IS THAT ONE INGREDIENT WORKS AGAINST THE OTHER: THE STARCH KEEPS THE TAPIOCA FROM BEING GUMMY AND THE TAPIOCA KEEPS THE STARCH FROM BEING CLOUDY. THE RESULT IS A SAUCE THAT ACTUALLY HAS A SPARKLE TO IT. THE MIXTURE HAS GREATER THICKENING POWER THAN CORNSTARCH ALONE, SO SLIGHTLY LESS SHOULD BE USED. A PASTE OF WATER AND FLOUR MAY ALSO BE USED TO THICKEN JUICES IN WHICH THERE IS ALREADY SOME OIL OR FAT, SUCH AS PAN DRIPPINGS. LIQUIDS IN WHICH THERE IS NO FAT MAY BE THICKENED BY THE CLASSIC "ROUX" OF BUTTER AND FLOUR, IN EQUAL PROPORTIONS. THIS MAY BE KNEADED TOGETHER INTO A BALL AND ADDED TO THE HOT LIQUID, OR BLENDED TOGETHER OVER LOW HEAT IN A PAN TO WHICH THE HOT LIQUID IS ADDED AND THEN STIRRED WITH A WHISK UNTIL THICK.

Black Mustard Seed Sauce

Put into blender and whirl for at
least 1 minute until completely
crushed:
1/2 cup black mustard seeds
4 tablespoons capers and juice
1/2 cup walnut oil
4 ounces melted butter

Then add and continue to blend:
4 ounces butter *(at room temperature)*

Thoroughly mix the ingredients
and pour into a container.

Use this sauce on top of halibut
to be broiled.

Variation for trout

4 parts mustard sauce
1 part Béarnaise sauce *(page 38)*

Hollandaise with Fresh Herbs

Bring to a full boil, making sure all
the butter is melted:
1/2 pound butter
1/4 cup lemon juice *(with enough
water added to make 2/3 cup liquid)*
2 sprigs tarragon
2 sprigs marjoram
2 sprigs lemon thyme
**4 leaves costmary or
2 sprigs mint**
1 leaf French sorrel

Heat blender with hot water.

Pour out water and put in:
3 egg yolks *(at room temperature)*
1/2 teaspoon gum tragacanth
*(optional, but it will help to keep the
sauce from separating)*

Start blender and immediately add
boiling butter mixture. Blend only
10 or 15 seconds, no more, or it
will not thicken properly. The beauty
of this method of making the sauce
is that it is quick, and the sauce will
hold up on the warm element of
an electric stove or over hot water in
a double boiler for an hour before
serving. If it starts to separate, a few
quick stirs with a wire whisk will
bring it together again.

Béarnaise Sauce

Cook over high heat until reduced to 2/3 its original volume:

1 cup white wine

1 tablespoon tarragon vinegar

1 tablespoon shallots, chopped fine *(green onions may be used)*

1 small sprig parsley, chopped fine

1 small sprig chervil or 2 tablespoons celery tops, chopped fine

2 small stalks tarragon

2 bruised peppercorns

When reduced, strain and return to pan, adding:

1/2 pound butter

Put into blender which has been heated with warm water:

3 egg yolks *(at room temperature)*

Heat butter and wine mixture until it begins to boil. Start blender whirling the egg yolks, and pour in immediately the wine and butter mixture. Whirl for about 10 seconds, just until it thickens; more will begin to thin it. If the butter and wine are not hot enough and the blender is not warm before the eggs go in, the sauce will not get thick; it is the slight cooking of the egg yolks that thickens it.

This sauce is best served at room temperature, which is the way Escoffier says it should be served. Do not try to serve it warm or it will separate. The present trend is to put meat glaze into it, which turns it gray, and then thicken it so it can be served warm. Horrible!

Ginger Sauce

Our chicken teriyaki has been liked so well that I thought we should try some other Hawaiian dishes. Of course the teriyaki sauce can be used to marinate any meat, and it is especially good for pork. However, I felt that since we were serving chicken in this style, I would fix the pork chops in a different way. I wanted to use the excellent combination of pineapple and ginger. One of the first things I discovered, as I experimented, is that fresh ginger that is sugared in one's own kitchen is far superior to any available in the stores, such as powdered ginger. It is very simple to fix — here is how to do it.

Soak ginger root in water for at least an hour, to make it easier to scrape, then cut off the little nubs or buds, and scrape clean:
1 pound ginger root *(fresh)*

Wash the scraped root clean and chop into thin pieces. Cook in very little water for 30 minutes, or until tender.

Add to ginger:
3 cups sugar
1 cup water
1 cup white corn syrup

Cook gently until flavor is blended. The addition of the corn syrup will prevent the crystallization of the sugar.

Pomegranate Sauce

Select the darkest colored, ripest fruit you can find. Try not to use the light pink pomegranates as their flavor is not so deep and rich as that of the fully matured ones.

Cut in half and juice as you would an orange:
pomegranates *(as many as you wish)*

When juicing the pomegranates, use side pressure against the juicer cone to extract all the juice. And watch out, for juice may fly in all directions! Reserve some of the seeds to use as a garnish; they are fine for adding interest and color.

Get at the market one of the prepared packages of:
pectin for jelly making

Follow the instructions on the package as you would for making berry jelly. The jelly may be a bit thick — you can stir or put it in the blender to thin it down if you wish.

This sauce is excellent served over ice cream or other desserts and is useful in salad dressings.

Sauce for Swiss Chard, Broccoli, & Similar Vegetables

Grind together:
2 leaves costmary
2 sprigs thyme
2 leaves French sorrel (*no stems*)
2 large leaves lovage
1/4 teaspoon herb salt

Mix with the herbs and cook until slightly thick:
1 cup water
2 tablespoons cornstarch
 (*dissolved in a little of the water*)
**2 vegetable or
 beef bouillon cubes**
1/4 cup yogurt
1/4 cup coffee cream

Add and stir in well:
**2 tablespoons strong
 horseradish**

Reheat to serving temperature. This sauce is excellent on all strong-flavored vegetables.

He even grows his own chard.

Lemon Cream Sauce

Melt:
8 ounces butter

Add, heat and stir until sugar dissolves:
1 1/2 cups sugar
1 1/2 cups lemon juice
zest from 1 lemon

Beat together and add to above:
3 whole eggs
3 egg yolks

Simmer the above until thick, then add:
1 cup heavy cream
 (*to desired consistency*)

Use on fruit crêpes.

Tomato Cream Sauce

Cook for about 5 minutes:
4 ounces butter
1 small yellow onion,
   chopped fine
1 carrot, chopped fine
1 large stalk celery,
   plus leaves, chopped

Add and simmer about 1 hour:
1 16–ounce can tomatoes
1 teaspoon herb salt
1/2 to 1 cup heavy cream

Puree in blender. To finish sauce, heat as needed. If sauce becomes too thick, thin with a little cream. Do not boil.

Dijon Mustard Sauce

This is a good sauce to be used with raw vegetables or as a garnish on salads.

Mix well together:
8 ounces sour cream
6 ounces cream cheese
2 teaspoons herb salt
1/2 teaspoon salad herbs
2 ounces Dijon mustard
1/2 teaspoon lemon juice
1/2 teaspoon caper juice
few drops yellow coloring
   (just for color)

Sauce Deauville

Boil until reduced to 2/3 cup:
1 cup white wine
2 tablespoons lemon or
   lime juice
2 teaspoons dill seed
1 teaspoon dill weed

When reduced, strain and add and heat until butter melts:
1/2 pound butter

Put into warmed blender top:
3 egg yolks

Start blender and add all at once, blending about 10 seconds:
boiling liquid *(from above)*

Remove from blender and stir in:
small amount of chopped,
   fresh dill weed

Serve over grilled fresh fish.

Brandy Sauce

Whip together well:
8 ounces butter
    (*at room temperature*)
3 cups sifted sugar
2 teaspoons stabilizer
    (*whipped cream type*)

When whipped to creamy
consistency add:
1 egg white

Beat again until creamy, then
add and fold in well:
4 tablespoons brandy
1 tablespoon whipping cream

Serve over hot pieces of pie.
A dash of fresh ground nutmeg
may be added to top it.

Serve at room temperature.

Pistachio Cream Sauce

Put into blender and whirl:
8 ounces shelled pistachios
1/4 cup sugar
1 1/2 cups coffee cream
1/4 teaspoon vanilla
2 drops green coloring

Heat to boiling to clear starch:
1 cup coffee cream
1/4 cup sugar
1/8 teaspoon salt
2 tablespoons starch

Add mixture from blender and
mix thoroughly.

Serve over coffee ice cream or
pot au crème.

Pesto Sauce

Whirl in blender until smooth:
1 1/2 cups basil,
    firmly packed
4 cloves garlic
1/4 cup pine nuts
1 cup olive oil
1 teaspoon salt
3/4 cup Parmesan
    cheese, grated

Rémoulade Sauce

Blend until thick:
1 cup Dijon mustard
1/2 cup paprika
2 teaspoon cayenne
4 tablespoons salt
2 cups vinegar
5 cups olive oil

Add and mix in thoroughly, but
do not blend:
4 cups green onions, minced
  (tops also)
2 cups celery, minced *(tops also)*
1 cup cilantro, minced

Make ahead of time to allow the
flavors to become well blended.

Creamed Horseradish Sauce

Whip until stiff but not buttery:
1/2 pint whipping cream
3/8 teaspoon gum tragacanth
  *(this stabilizes the sauce so
  it will not get soft)*

Add and fold in gently:
**4 tablespoons strong
  horseradish** *(use the type
  that says strong on the label)*
1/4 teaspoon lemon juice
3/8 teaspoon herb salt

This is good on any type of beef,
especially roast prime rib and
old-fashioned boiled beef.

Béchamel Sauce

Combine in a saucepan:
4 tablespoons butter
8 tablespoons flour

Add, cook and stir until just thick:
1 cup whole milk
1 cup coffee cream
1 bay leaf *(discard when cooked)*

Mix together:
3 tablespoons white wine
1 1/2 teaspoons lemon juice
1/2 teaspoon herb salt

Add wine-lemon juice mixture to
the sauce, stirring well.

Tennessee Chili Jelly

Our friends, the Bakers, invited us to dinner one evening and the first thing my eye lighted on at the table was a dish of jelly that had a lovely pink color. It was a special gift for this occasion, my hostess said, brought by the lady who helped to serve, and the recipe came from the hills of Tennessee. It had a special flavor, made from the juice of sweet red chilies, not hot, but unusual. Try it! Here is the recipe:

Chop and cook gently for about
10 minutes:
6 large sweet red peppers
6 cups water

When done, pour into a cloth bag and hang to drain overnight.
Do not squeeze the bag or the juice will be cloudy. Next day make the jelly according to directions on a package of:
Certo, using the drained juice

Turmeric Corn Relish

Put in boiling water and cook for
2 minutes, counting only when the water starts to boil again:
9 ears corn

Cut, then scrape the corn from the cob.

Blend in a large bowl:
1 teaspoon turmeric
1 tablespoon dry
   ground mustard
2 teaspoons celery seeds
4 tablespoons salt

Pour in and stir until dry ingredients are dissolved:
2 cups cider vinegar
1 cup light brown sugar

Mix in, then simmer gently for
30 minutes:
the corn kernels
3 cups minced fresh cabbage
1/2 cup chopped celery
2 small onions, minced
1 green pepper, minced
1 sweet red pepper, minced

Have hot sterilized jars ready; fill and seal immediately.

Makes 5 or 6 pints

Fresh Apricot Chutney

In Ojai where we live, in the late spring we can get wonderful, fresh non-irrigated apricots, smaller in size than the commercially grown ones so that the flavor is concentrated. With these we make chutney.

Cut in quarters but do not peel:
**3 pounds apricots, slightly on
    the green side**

Add and cook until almost but not quite soft:
**3 1/2 pounds light brown sugar
4 cloves garlic, minced
1/2 red chili, Mexican type**
    *(not the small Japanese ones), (pounded
    or run dry in the blender for 5 minutes
    until chopped fine)*
**1/4 pound fresh ginger root
    that has been soaked,
    scraped and sliced**

Add and cook for 30 minutes:
**2 1/2 cups vinegar
1 1/2 pounds seedless raisins
2 teaspoons salt
1 teaspoon powdered cinnamon
1/6 teaspoon powdered cloves
1/6 teaspoon powdered
    cardamom
3/8 teaspoon cayenne pepper**

Add after cooking:
**1/2 cup fresh lemon or
    lime juice** *(to give extra tartness
    and fresh flavor)*

This chutney will keep for months in a covered crock and in a cool place. But it won't last that long if you let anybody taste it!

*There are
several ways
that sauces can
be thickened.*

Italian Chestnut Dressing

Cut a 1/2–inch cross in 2 cups Italian chestnuts. Roast in 400° oven for 20 minutes. Remove and as soon as they can be handled, remove outer shell and inner skin. Cut into fourths. This should make about 1 cup peeled meat.

Put into pressure cooker and cook for 30 minutes at 15 pounds pressure:
gizzard, neck and heart of fowl
1 1/2 cups water

When cooked, reserve broth and remove meat from neck bones and chop fine with gizzard and heart.

Put into mixing bowl:
1 cup onions, sliced thin
1 cup celery, sliced thin
1/4 cup parsley, chopped fine
1 cup prepared chestnuts
meat from gizzard , neck
**   and heart**

Add and stir in well but do not make mushy:
1 cup broth from cooking fowl

Put into baking dish and bake for 45 minutes at 350° until bread begins to brown, uncovered.

Serve with gravy from roasted fowl. This is excellent with roasted turkey, duck or goose.

APPETIZERS, BREADS & SPREADS

We all ordered the same dish.

I'VE INCLUDED RECIPES FOR APPETIZERS, SUCH AS OUR RANCH HOUSE PATÉ WITH COGNAC SPREADS, GREEN CRUNCH, AND SEVERAL RECIPES FOR DELICIOUS BREADS. I HAVE DELIBERATELY NOT INCLUDED MOST OF OUR BREAD RECIPES HERE (YOU CAN FIND THEM IN MY BOOK, *Vegetarian Gourmet Cookery*) BUT I WOULD LIKE TO SAY A FEW WORDS ABOUT WHAT, FOR ME, IS LITERALLY THE STAFF OF LIFE.

OUR WHOLE WHEAT BREAD, WHICH WE MADE OURSELVES AND SERVED IN THE OLD RANCH HOUSE, HAD BECOME SO POPULAR THAT WE DECIDED TO CONTINUE

MAKING IT. WE SET UP A SMALL BAKERY IN THE BACK ROOM OF MY PARENTS' HOME TWO BLOCKS AWAY, AND INCREASED THE VARIETY OF HOMEMADE BREADS. LATER, WE MOVED THIS LITTLE BAKING OPERATION INTO THE KITCHEN OF THE NEW RESTAURANT. THUS THE THREAD OF FLAVORFULLY DELICIOUS HOMEMADE BREAD HAS NEVER BEEN BROKEN SINCE WE BEGAN IT IN 1950. GUESTS AT THE RANCH HOUSE STILL GO INTO THE KITCHEN TO SELECT THEIR SUPPLY OF FRESH, "HOME BAKED" LOAVES TO TAKE AWAY WITH THEM.

WHEAT IS NEARLY A COMPLETE FOOD. WE MAKE OUR WHOLE WHEAT BREAD WITH THE MOST SIMPLE RECIPE — STONE-GROUND, WHOLE WHEAT FLOUR, MILK, BUTTER, HONEY, YEAST AND SALT; ISN'T THAT UNCOMPLICATED ENOUGH? THE WHEATY TASTE IS ALL THERE, WITH NO ADDITIVES TO COVER IT UP. FOR OUR WHITE BREAD WE USE NOTHING BUT UNBLEACHED WHITE FLOUR AND AS MUCH SOYA FLOUR AS IT WILL TAKE TO STAND AND STILL RISE TO THE PROPER HEIGHT. WE ALSO MAKE 100 PERCENT RYE (WHICH IS HARD AND QUITE STICKY AND GETS ALL OVER YOUR HANDS IN THE FIRST MIXING), OATMEAL, AND DATE-NUT BREADS.

Ranch House Paté
with Cognac

A ballerina, Carmeleta Maracci, gave me this recipe. I have modified it a little.

Braise only until clear, do not brown:
**4 green onions, including
   tops, chopped fine, in
   4 tablespoons butter**

Add and cook for 10 minutes, covered:
1 1/4 pounds chicken livers
   (goose livers may be used)

Mix together and add to livers:
**2 teaspoons salt
2 teaspoons dry mustard
1/2 teaspoon fresh ground
   nutmeg
1/4 teaspoon ground cloves**

Run mixture in blender at high speed for 2 minutes, then add and run again, stirring at least twice:
**1/4 pound butter
8 ounces Philadelphia
   cream cheese
1/4 cup cognac**

You may also add:
truffles

The truffles should be chopped and added after the paté is removed from the blender. Chill for at least 24 hours before serving. The paté can be put into attractive little dishes, garnished with a slice of truffle and stored. *(There are those who will consider the addition of the cream cheese a sacrilege, but it smooths the paté so beautifully that we disregard the purists.)*

*A ballerina gave
me this recipe.*

Greek Dolmas

Mix the following ingredients together:
1/4 tablespoon herb salt
2 cups onion, minced
1/2 cup long-grain rice, uncooked
1/3 cup olive oil
2 tablespoons parsley, minced
1 tablespoon dill weed
1/4 cup pine nuts
1/4 cup currents, soaked in white wine
1 cup lamb, minced

Prepare:
grape leaves

Put 2 tablespoons of the above ingredients on each grape leaf and roll tightly. Poach in beef stock with a little lemon juice and fresh mint for 1 1/2 hours.

Serve hot or cold with:
sour cream and chutney

(Dolmas may be made vegetarian by leaving out the minced lamb and poaching them in a vegetable stock with lemon and mint.)

Makes 50 dolmas

Stuffed Mushroom Caps

Braise:
2 tablespoons butter
4 cloves garlic, minced
1 onion, minced

Add and mix in well:
1 cup almonds, toasted well and ground
1 cup hazelnuts, toasted and ground
1 teaspoon herb salt
mushroom stems, chopped and braised
2 eggs, beaten

Broil mushroom caps, stuff with above mixture, and put under broiler until browned on top.

Greek Vegetable Antipasto

Prepare the following dressing.

Mix together well:
**2 cups Ranch House salad
    dressing** (*Italian wine vinegar*)
1/2 cup lemon juice
1/4 cup oregano, minced
1/2 cup parsley, minced
2 teaspoons herb salt

Prepare the following vegetables first:
2 bunches green onions, minced
    (*using half the length of the green tops*)
**1/2 basket cherry tomatoes,
    cut in half**
2 small zucchini, sliced thin
1 sweet red pepper, sliced
1 sweet green pepper, sliced
1 yellow sweet pepper, sliced
    (*if available*)
2 cups pitted olives
2 cups artichokes, quartered
    (*canned*)
**8 ounces Feta cheese,
    cut into 1/2–inch cubes**

Then marinate them in the dressing
for at least 30 minutes with:
**4 cups mushrooms, washed
    and sliced**

To serve:
Lay lettuce leaf on chilled plate.
Mound 1/2 cup antipasto on lettuce.
Cut into strips some pickled red
sweet peppers out of a jar and lay
2 strips crosswise on top of vegetable
mixture. Put 2 half cherry tomatoes
between each corner of the red
peppers for color.

Snails au Crème

To prepare snails that have been farm raised or properly purged, rinse lightly in fresh water:
72 snails (*12 per order*)

Bring to a boil:
6 quarts water
1/2 cup apple cider vinegar
1 tablespoon salt

Add snails and boil for 15 minutes. Then drain, shell, and rinse well with cold water.

In another pan place:
3 1/2 cups white wine
1 carrot
1 stalk celery
1 onion, peeled
and a bouquet garni
   wrapped in cheese of:
   10 whole cloves
   3 bay leaves
   6 sprigs parsley
   8 cloves garlic
snails from above
enough water to cover
   the snails

Cover and simmer very gently for 1 1/4 hours. When done, remove snails and refrigerate.

In a large non-stick skillet, add and sauté until it reduces and starts to thicken:
2 tablespoons butter
4 teaspoons garlic, minced
2 cups heavy cream
2 tablespoons white wine
1/4 teaspoon white pepper
1 1/2 teaspoons herb salt
2 tablespoons parsley, chopped

When done, add the above snails and cook until heated through. Serve with sautéed oyster or shitake mushrooms.

Serves 6

Ah, escargot!

Snails with Pesto

To prepare snails that have been farm raised or properly purged, rinse lightly in fresh water:
72 snails (*12 per order*)

Bring to a boil:
6 quarts water
1/2 cup apple cider vinegar
1 tablespoon salt

Add snails and boil for 15 minutes. Then drain, shell, and rinse well with cold water.

In another pan place:
3 1/2 cups white wine
8 cloves garlic
1 bunch parsley
snails from above
enough water to cover
    the snails

Cover and simmer very gently for 1 1/4 hours. When done, remove snails and refrigerate.

In a large non–stick skillet add and sauté:
2 tablespoons butter
1 cup fresh pesto

Then add the above snails and cook until heated through. Serve with toast points which have been spread with herbed goat cheese.

Serves 6

Crab Puffs

Mix together completely:
1 1/4 cups mayonnaise
5/8 teaspoon garlic salt
1 teaspoon curry powder
1 pound cooked and
    shredded crab meat

Then fold in gently:
3 large egg whites (*beaten stiff*)

Spread mixture on crackers and put under broiler until lightly brown. Serve immediately.

Oysters on the Half Shell

Prepare oysters (*opening them*) and lay at least 2 on each opened shell. At the side in a small dish, put the following sauce.

Mix together until smooth:
2 cups Béarnaise sauce (*page 38*)
1 cup Dijon mustard
2 tablespoons lemon juice
1 teaspoon horseradish
1 teaspoon honey

Garnish each oyster in shell with small round of pimento after laying oysters on a bed of lettuce. Serve very cold.

Caviar Caper

This dish is best made in a stainless steel or glass baking pan (*9 by 11 1/2 inches*) so it can be removed for easy serving. Bring to a boil, stirring constantly:
3 cups water
1/2 cup cucumber juice
     (*purée cucumber in blender and strain for juice*)
3 packets Knox gelatin
3/4 teaspoon sugar

Cool to room temperature.

In baking pan make 1 layer of each:
3/4 cup red onions, minced
8 hard boiled eggs, minced

Pour the cucumber–gelatin mixture over the onions and eggs, being careful not to disturb the layers. Refrigerate for 4 hours until firm.

Now turn upside down on serving platter and place hot towels on bottom of pan to unmold. Cut into 1-inch square serving pieces and top with the following mixture.

In mixer beat until smooth and fluffy:
2 ounces cream cheese
1 ounce whipping cream

When ready to serve, top with your favorite caviar.

Oysters Rockefeller

Shuck and reserve liquid:
2 dozen oysters

Sauté:
3/4 pound sweet butter
4 teaspoons garlic, minced
1 1/2 teaspoons salt
1/4 teaspoon cayenne
3 tablespoons anchovy paste
3 cups coarsely chopped parsley
1 1/2 cups coarsely chopped
scallions (tops also)
1 1/2 pounds fresh spinach,
patted dry, cut into
1–inch pieces
3 cups clam juice (include liquid
from above oysters)

When done stir in:
3/4 cup Pernod

Lay oysters on shells. Spoon
the parsley mixture over them. Put
under broiler until very hot and
serve immediately.

Ham & Cheese Feuillete

On a suitable pan that can be put in
the refrigerator, lay a sheet of puff
pastry (10 by 15 inches). On this,
spread evenly, leaving 1/2 inch from
the edge bare:
1/4 cup Dijon mustard

On top of the mustard place the
following, in alternating layers:
1 pound ham, sliced thin
1/4 pound Swiss cheese,
sliced thin
1/4 pound Provolone,
sliced thin

Wet the bare edges of the pastry
with water and lay on top another
sheet of pastry. Fold over the edges
and crimp evenly with a fork to seal.
Brush on top the following, which
has been beaten together:
1 egg
1 teaspoon cream

Cut off any excess pastry at edges of
sheet. Let stand in refrigerator until
dry. Remove from refrigerator and
coat once again with egg mixture.
Bake at 400° until golden brown. Cut
into serving squares (2 by 2 inches).

Serve hot.

Baby Abalone & Alassio Sauce

Make the following sauce.

Cook until just done but not mushy:
1/2 cup olive oil
2 cups celery, minced
1 carrot, minced
1 1/2 bell peppers, minced
5 green onions, minced
1/2 teaspoon fish herb blend
1/2 teaspoon herb salt

When done add and heat to serving temperature:
2 tablespoons lemon juice
1/2 cup Béchamel sauce (*page 43*)
**1 1/2 cups crab meat,
    chopped fine**

To serve, sauté abalone in butter very quickly on each side.

Serve immediately on the above sauce which has been spread over a bed of rice. Garnish lightly with finely chopped parsley and lime wedge.

Smoked Trout Pasta Cream

In a large saucepan combine and simmer until reduced and slightly thickened:
6 cups whipping cream
1 cup white wine
1/4 cup lime juice
1 teaspoon herb salt
1 minced red onion
**4 tablespoons minced
    fresh dill weed**
1/4 teaspoon white pepper

When done remove from heat and add:
**3 cups peeled and seeded
    tomatoes, chopped**
**4 sides smoked trout,
    chopped**

Serve with angel hair pasta garnished with smoked shrimp.

Banana-Apricot
Nut Bread

Cream together:
1/3 cup butter
  (at room temperature)
2/3 cup sugar

Add and beat well:
2 eggs

Mix together:
**1 cup sliced medium–ripe
  bananas**
1/4 cup buttermilk

Sift together:
1 1/4 cups sifted flour
1/2 teaspoon salt
**1 teaspoon Royal baking
  powder**
**1/2 teaspoon powdered
  cardamom**
1/2 teaspoon baking soda

Add banana mixture and flour
mixture alternately to egg mixture,
then stir in:
1 cup whole bran
3/4 cup dried apricots, chopped
1/2 cup walnuts, chopped

Put into 9 by 5 by 3-inch greased
pan and bake at 375° for 1 hour or
until done. Cool on wire rack.

Surrulitos de Maiz

Mix together:
1 cup cornmeal
1 teaspoon garlic salt
1 teaspoon sea salt
  (available at health food stores)
1 teaspoon cilantro, minced
1 tablespoon butter
1 vegetable bouillon cube
1 1/4 cups water

If the cornmeal is coarse, use a
little less water. Cook until mixture
thickens, stirring constantly, then
lower heat and cook for 15 to 20
minutes, stirring once or twice. Set
aside to cool a little, then mix in:
**2 generous tablespoons
  grated Parmesan cheese**

When the mush is cool enough to
handle, put a heaping tablespoon in
the palm of your hand and form it
into a ball; then roll it between the
palms to make the *surrulito* about
2 inches long. In Puerto Rico these
are fried, but they are most delicious
baked. Put a small amount of oil on
a cookie sheet and roll each surrulito
in it as you arrange them on a sheet.

Bake at 350° until they are brown on
top, then turn them over. They can
also be cooked under the broiler if
watched carefully and broiled on
both sides to get deliciously brown
and crisp. They can be frozen for
future use.

California Spice Bread

Several years ago my friend Martha Agnew mentioned that sometime I should experiment with a bread she called Pain des Épices. I thought of it now and then but never seemed to get around to doing anything about it. Then another friend, Torre Taggart, returned from living in India, bringing talk and recipes from faraway lands. Now was the time to try the spice bread recipe. I have brought the East and West together in this recipe, adding soy flour which is not generally used in India. Here is the tested recipe, and I think the only difficulty you will have will be to prevent its being entirely consumed before the loaf has a chance to cool.

Sift before measuring:
3/4 cup soy flour

Mix with flour and heat to lukewarm, about 90°:
1/4 cup wheat germ
2 teaspoons salt
1 tablespoon butter
1/4 cup honey
3/4 cup water
1 cup whole milk

Add to lukewarm mixture and stir in well:
2 packages dry yeast
2 teaspoons powdered
 cardamom seeds
2 teaspoons powdered
 coriander seeds
1 teaspoon nutmeg
1/4 teaspoon allspice

Let stand at least 15 minutes so that yeast can reconstitute, making the mixture frothy. Then with large spoon stir in:

2 cups white
 unbleached flour
 (sifted before measuring)

RANCH HOUSE

Our bread had become so popular.

Nut Bread

When this is well mixed in, add and continue to mix:
2 cups white unbleached flour
(sifted before measuring)

To get all of the flour mixed in, turn the dough out on a lightly floured board and knead it. Continue the kneading until the dough is smooth and springy.

Put in a bowl to rise, smooth side up, until double its bulk, perhaps 30 minutes. Turn out on the floured board and knead again for another 10 minutes or so, to give it a good texture. Divide the dough in half and knead and shape each piece into a log, folding the ends under so that the top will have a smooth surface skin. There must be no breaks in the top or the loaf will burst open when baking.

Put the logs into small, well-buttered bread tins and let rise to about 1/2 inch above the rim of the pan. Bake at 360° for 35 minutes.

When baked, remove from pans and put on wire cooling rack or stand on end; otherwise the surface of the loaf will sweat and become wet and soft. The top may be brushed with butter, but this is not necessary.

Beat lightly in mixing bowl:
1 egg

Add, and beat with egg:
1 1/2 cups lukewarm milk
1 tablespoon melted butter
1 teaspoon vanilla

Sift together, then mix well into liquid:
4 cups all-purpose
**   white flour, sifted**
1 cup sugar
1 teaspoon salt
1/4 teaspoon allspice
4 teaspoons Royal
**   baking powder**

Add and mix well:
1 cup walnuts,
**   coarsely chopped**

Let stand for 15 minutes, then bake at 325° for 1 hour in large, greased loaf pan. Cool on wire rack.

Orange Cream Filling

Whip in mixer for 2 minutes or until smooth:
8 ounces cream cheese
3 ounces orange concentrate

Add, and continue to whip:
2 tablespoons honey
1/8 teaspoon powdered cardamon

Chill filling before using. Use as a sandwich spread on date nut bread. Use for a sandwich plate with cottage cheese and fresh fruit.

Fresh Coconut-Ginger Bread

Mix together in a pan:
1/2 cup warm water
2 1/4 cups fresh coconut milk
   (the coconut milk can be made by running in the blender for 5 minutes 1 cup of hot water and 1/2 cup grated fresh coconut meat (then repeat, using the same portions); or coconut milk may be obtained frozen and completely defrosted before using)

Add to coconut milk and water:
1 tablespoon butter
1/3 cup honey
2 teaspoons salt
1 tablespoon fresh ginger root, grated *(more if desired)*

Heat to 90°, about body temperature, then add and stir in:
2 packages dry yeast

Let stand until yeast dissolves and little bubbles begin to appear. Then add and mix in well, first with a spoon, then by hand to get in all the flour:
6 2/3 cups whole–wheat flour, sifted
   (accurate measurements are important; 5 3/4 cups unsifted flour equals 6 2/3 cups sifted flour)
1 cup grated fresh coconut

Pimento Cheese Spread

Knead until dough is thoroughly mixed. It should be moist and slightly sticky. Cover with a cloth and set in a warm place to rise to double its bulk. This will take 15 to 20 minutes.

Turn out onto a floured board and knead again for at least 10 minutes, pressing the dough down flat, folding it over and turning it around until the large air bubbles are squeezed out. This will make a good texture. Dough should be springy to the touch, good and tough.

Cut the dough into 2 equal parts. Flatten each piece out and fold over. Repeat this flattening and folding until, when rolled up, each piece forms a log the size of the pan.

Grease the pans with shortening (*butter will burn and the bread will stick to the pan*). When the dough is put into the pan, be sure the upper part is smooth and unbroken; a break will make the dough break out in bubbles. Let rise until dough is about 1 inch higher than the rim of the pan. Bake at 375° for 45 minutes. Turn out on rack to cool.

Sometimes you need to make a lot of sandwiches quickly. Here is a recipe for 50 delicious sandwiches that can be made without fuss or bother.

Whip in mixer until light and fluffy:
1 1/2 pounds Philadelphia cream cheese
1 1/2 pounds butter
   (*at room temperature*)
1 1/2 teaspoons herb salt

Add and whip 1/2 minute, just until incorporated:
3 7–ounce cans pimentos, chopped

Minced Chicken Filling

Mince:
2 cups cooked chicken

Salt lightly with:
herb salt

Add, mix well and chill:
**1/2 cup celery hearts
    and leaves, chopped
3/4 cup mayonnaise
1/4 cup sour cream
1/4 cup almonds, toasted
    and sliced**

As a variation, add 1 or both:
**parsley, minced fine
pimentos, chopped
    fine**

Curried Egg

Boil, cool and peel, then slice thin:
4 eggs

Mix together:
**1/2 cup mayonnaise
1/2 teaspoon curry powder
2 teaspoons mustard**
    (the type made with horseradish is best)
**1/2 teaspoon herb salt
1 teaspoon chutney, mashed fine**

Mix with egg slices. This is good on any type of bread.

Lunch for two.

Green Crunch

Stir or whip until smooth:

**8 ounces Philadelphia
cream cheese**
2 ounces mayonnaise
**1 teaspoon Worcestershire
sauce**

Mix together:

**4 green onions, tops included,
chopped fine or coarse**
(*as you wish*)
**1 green pepper, chopped into
1/4–inch pieces**
**1 sweet red pepper, chopped
into 1/4–inch pieces**
**2 tablespoons green celery,
chopped fine**

Mix cheese and chopped vegetables.
Spread on unbuttered bread just
before serving, so that the bread will
not get soggy.

Steamed Mussels & Pasta

In a saucepan with a trivet in the
bottom, to keep the mussels above
the liquid, add:

1 cup cream (*half and half*)
1 1/2 teaspoons tarragon
1 clove garlic, minced

Wash any mud or sand off the
mussels and cut the hair off with
scissors. Do not soak in water or
they will open up and die. The
shells should be firmly closed.

Put the mussels on the trivet (*about
20*) and cover the pan tight. Simmer
for about 5 minutes or until all
mussels open. When done remove
mussels from pan and serve on
fresh pasta which has been tossed
in the following sauce.

In a small saucepan add:

1 cup cream (*half and half*)
1 1/2 teaspoons tarragon
1 clove garlic minced
3/4 teaspoon herb salt

Bring to a simmer on low heat and
thicken slightly with flour dissolved
in water. Remove from heat and add:

1/4 cup sour cream

Toss with hot prepared pasta.

Olive-Tomato Appetizer

Prepare a marinade by mixing together:
3/4 cup olive oil
3 tablespoons wine vinegar
juice of 1/2 lemon
10 turns of the pepper mill

Pour marinade over:
3 medium cans pitted black olives, drained

Marinate olives in refrigerator for 5 hours. One hour before serving, mix in gently:
2 cups cherry tomatoes, sliced in half

Continue to chill until ready to serve. Drain off marinade and serve in large relish bowl placed in crushed ice. Have toothpicks available. This is excellent served with champagne cocktails.

SOUPS

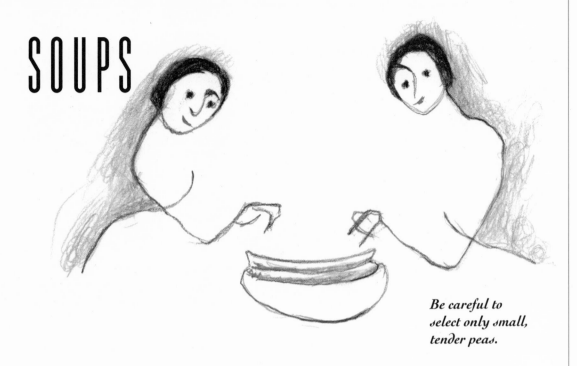

Be careful to select only small, tender peas.

You may notice as you read the soup recipes and the sauce recipes that there is very little mention of the stockpot. During years of cooking without meat, I had to learn how to make tasty and hearty sauces and soups without depending on meat broths as a flavoring foundation. (Why accept that only chicken or veal stock will make a rich cream soup?) With suitable herbs and spices one learns to enhance the natural flavor of whatever vegetable is used to make the soup, or whatever ingredients are used to make the sauce. Without such knowledge the vegetarian diet would be bleak indeed!

Texture, so important in other dishes, is no less important to soup. Finely cut and lightly cooked vegetables, added to the soup for texture, will also impart extraordinary freshness, especially in soups made with a clear or semi-clear broth. Cream soups do not need much thickening; some need none at all.

Selecting the best herb for a soup depends somewhat on whether it is a clear soup, a thick soup, a cream soup or a chilled soup. But the dominant

FLAVOR OF THE SOUP BEFORE HERBS ARE ADDED DICTATES WHICH ONES ARE TO BE USED.

FRESH HERBS ARE ALWAYS BEST, BUT THE DRIED ONES ARE QUITE GOOD ALSO. THEY SHOULD BE FIRST GROUND IN A MORTAR SO THAT THEIR FLAVORS WILL MARRY WITH THE FLAVOR OF THE SOUP. HAVING LARGE PIECES OF HERBS FLOATING IN THE SOUP IS NOT RECOMMENDED EXCEPT FOR SPECIAL THINGS LIKE FRESH WATERCRESS.

REMEMBER THAT CREAM SOUPS SHOULD BE DELICATELY FLAVORED, CHICKEN A BIT STRONGER, AND BEEF OR LAMB CAN HAVE A STILL STRONGER ACCENT OF HERBS.

SOME SOUPS ACCUMULATE; OTHERS ARE ALWAYS MADE FROM SCRATCH. ALL JUICES FROM COOKED VEGETABLES SHOULD BE FAITHFULLY SAVED AND STORED IN THE REFRIGERATOR; ALL SCRAPS OF VEGETABLES THAT ARE STILL FRESH SHOULD LIKEWISE BE SAVED AND STORED IN A PLASTIC BAG OR HUMIDIFIER. SAVE ALL MEAT BROTHS AND BONES, FOR BOUILLON. MOST SOUPS REHEAT THE NEXT DAY, EXCELLENTLY. HEAT THEM IN A DOUBLE BOILER TO PREVENT SCORCHING.

SOUPS USUALLY FALL INTO ONE OF THE FOLLOWING CATEGORIES: 1. SLIGHTLY SWEET, SUCH AS CORN, GREEN PEA, GREEN BEAN, CELERY, AND SO ON; 2. WITH MEAT BROTHS OR TOMATO JUICE – FRENCH SORREL IS ONE OF THESE; 3. THICK SOUPS, SUCH AS YELLOW OR GREEN SPLIT PEA, POTATO, BLACK BEAN, PARSLEY, GARBANZO, LENTIL, AND SO ON.

THE FIRST GROUP IS MADE FROM A VEGETABLE WITH A DELICATE FLAVOR WHICH MUST NOT BE OVERSHADOWED BY ANOTHER FLAVOR. THE SECOND SHOULD HAVE PLENTY OF LIQUID – SOMETHING THAT IS SOMETIMES FORGOTTEN IN THE PREPARATION. IN THE THIRD GROUP, THE LEGUMES SHOULD BE VERY WELL DONE, SO THAT THEY CAN BE TURNED INTO A WONDERFUL, THICK LIQUID WHICH CAN BE ROLLED ON THE TONGUE FOR TASTING. MANY OF THESE ARE MADE BY PUTTING THE COOKED VEGETABLES THROUGH THE BLENDER.

Chicken Gumbo Soup

At various times I lived in New Orleans where I acquired a taste for gumbo and have loved it ever since. Some people do not like gumbo the first time they taste it. But if you will try it a few times, you will probably learn to love it too.

You will need to get gumbo filé for this soup, and be sure you have the authentic New Orleans variety, which contains powdered sassafras and a little thyme. Chicken or turkey gizzards or pieces of either can be used in this soup. The gizzards make a wonderful rich broth.

Simmer covered for 1/2 hour:
**3/4 pound chicken or
    turkey gizzards
2 cups water**

Add, and simmer for 1 1/2 hours:
**5 pounds chicken or
    turkey necks and backs
4 cups water** (*add more water,
    if necessary, as broth is cooking*)

Strain broth, allow to cool and skim off fat. Remove skin and bones from chicken; then chop chicken meat and gizzards fine and reserve. Combine and simmer about 1/2 hour, or until vegetables are tender:
**2 cups of the chicken broth
3/4 cup celery, cut fine
1/2 cup onions, chopped fine
2 tablespoons parsley,
    chopped fine**

2 bay leaves (*very essential;
    discard when cooked*)
**1/4 teaspoon salt
1/8 teaspoon paprika
1/2 tablespoon sugar
3 chicken bouillon cubes
1/8 teaspoon black pepper
1 16-ounce can tomatoes,
    mashed**

Add and cook until cornstarch clears:
**1 1/2 tablespoons cornstarch,
    dissolved in a little water**

Now add, stirring the mixture well, and skim if necessary:
1 28-ounce can okra, drained
    (*or 2 cups fresh, cooked okra*)
**4 cups water
2 cups of the chicken broth
the reserved chopped chicken
    or turkey
1/2 cup cooked ham, minced**

Add, stirring in quickly and using wire whisk, for the powder may get into little balls if not quickly whisked into the liquid:
2 tablespoons gumbo filé

Heat again and skim off any fat that comes to the top. Do not boil, as the gumbo then becomes slimy because of the okra.

Serves 6

Barbecued Chicken Soup

The first time Paul Newman and his wife Joanne Woodward came to the Ranch House, we had this soup. He said, "I'll try it — but how can you barbecue a soup?" He liked it.

Most markets nowadays have electric barbecue machines in connection with their meat departments. Take a plastic container that has a cover and ask your butcher to reserve for you some of the broth that comes from the chicken as it is being barbecued.

Ask him to save only the chicken drippings, not a mixture of sauces from other barbecued meats. If you bring home too much sauce, part of it can be frozen for future use. You will find that this sauce is very salty and rich; it must be diluted for your soup.

Proceed little by little in mixing the sauce and the water until the mixture satisfies your taste requirements. You will need a quart of the mixture for this recipe.

Cook in pressure cooker without cap for 1 minute, or steam in covered pan until vegetables are tender–crisp:

1/2 cup water
1 small onion, minced
1/4 green pepper, minced
1 small stalk celery, minced
1/2 zucchini, minced
1/2 teaspoon soup herb blend
1 bay leaf (*discard when cooked*)
1 tablespoon lemon juice

Add cooked vegetables to diluted barbecue sauce and heat to serving temperature.

Serves 4

Mexican Chicken Soup

This is an easy soup to make, almost as simple as the barbecued chicken soup recipe. Actually, it is a variation of that recipe, although quite different in taste.

Prepare a rich chicken broth by simmering for 1 1/2 hours:
**5 pounds chicken necks
and/or backs**
4 cups water

Drain, skim and reserve broth. Discard skin, take meat from bones, chop fine and reserve.

Cook in pressure cooker without the cap, for 1 minute only, or steam in covered pan until vegetables are tender–crisp:
1/4 cup water
1 chicken bouillon cube
1 small onion, minced
1/4 green pepper, minced
1 small stalk celery, minced
1/2 zucchini, minced
1 teaspoon soup herb blend
1 bay leaf (*discard when cooked*)

Mix together:
4 cups chicken broth
    (*add water to broth if needed*)
1 1/2 tablespoons cilantro, minced
3/4 tablespoon beef stock concentrate
1 tablespoon lemon juice
salt to taste
chopped chicken meat

Heat to serving temperature and garnish with:
1 avocado, cubed
pinch of cilantro (*optional*)

Serves 6

Authentic Vietnamese Soup

This is another of the recipes given me by Mr. So, the Chinese gentleman from Vietnam whose recipe which we call Beef Bali Hai is given in the section on meats. On the last night of my visit to Paris, he invited us for a special dinner which he prepared himself. It was another evening as delightful as the first one had been. I listened most sympathetically as he reminisced about his struggle to establish himself in Paris. His first restaurant, he told us, was just ten feet wide, with little tables along one wall, a tiny kitchen, and a second floor of the same size. Students from the nearby Sorbonne flocked to the tiny restaurant for the delicious Vietnamese dishes he served. Here is the soup he gave us that night.

Prepare a rich broth, by simmering for 1 1/2 hours:
**5 pounds chicken necks,
    backs and wings**
4 cups water

Strain, skim and reserve broth and the meat from the chicken.
Mix together:
1 cup cooked rice
1 cup flaked crab meat
1 teaspoon cilantro
**1 teaspoon herb salt or
    1 chicken bouillon cube**
    (salt to taste if cube is used)
meat from chicken parts
4 cups chicken broth
    (add water to broth if needed)

Heat to serving temperature and garnish with:
fresh cilantro, finely chopped

Serves 6

Baked Potato Soup

Potatoes are such a staple food. In Europe, especially Germany and England, to say nothing about Ireland, they are eaten three times a day.

This recipe, Baked Potato Soup, has been one of the most popular soups we have ever served, mostly because the flavor comes from the baked skins. Someone wrote some time ago, "Even the potato has a low form of cunning," or how else could its popularity be accounted for? Nutritionally it is supposed to have a variety of minerals and vitamins. Viva La Potato.

Remove any black pieces from:
10 cold baked potatoes

Remove skins leaving 1/8 to 1/4 of potato center; discard the rest.

Put into blender:
1 quart hot water
4 vegetable bouillon cubes
1 medium onion
    sautéed in 1 stick butter
    (4 ounces)
potato skins

While blending add:
1/2 gallon whole milk

Heat to serving temperature over water.

Garnish with:
chopped red onions
grated Cheddar cheese

Soup of the Casbah

Although Charles Boyer denied saying, "Take me to the Casbah," I think he might have said it if he had heard that in one of those little hole-in-the-wall restaurants they were serving this soup, sopped up with plenty of dark, hearty bread! But if you can't get away to this mysterious place, you can try it in less adventurous circumstances, right in your own home.

Braise in an open pan in 400° oven for about 30 minutes until meat is nicely browned, to get that dark–brown taste:
4 pounds lamb neck,
   cut into 4 pieces

Put browned lamb in pressure cooker with 4 cups of water and cook for 30 minutes at 15 pounds pressure, or simmer in covered kettle for several hours. When done, remove meat from bones and chop fine. Allow broth to cool, skim off fat and add chopped meat.

Add and cook for 20 minutes at 15 pounds pressure, or until vegetables are tender in a covered kettle:
1 onion, chopped fine
2 stalks celery, chopped fine
1 green pepper, chopped fine
1 large carrot, chopped fine
1 clove garlic, chopped fine
1 1/4 cups lentils
1 bay leaf (*discard when cooked*)
4 cups water
3 tablespoons beef base

Garnish with:
paper–thin slices of fresh lime
   or a dollop of yogurt

Serves 6

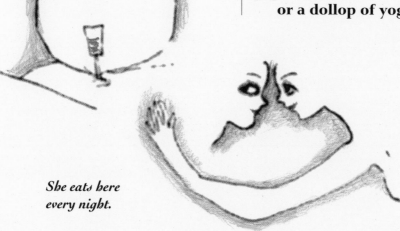

She eats here
every night.

Oxtail with Barley

My English-born grandmother lived with us when I was young. She was a superb cook and one of her specialties was soup. Here is one of her recipes using that wonderful grain, barley, which somehow seems to have gone out of fashion. This recipe may revive your interest in barley and put extra nourishment in the stomachs of those to whom you serve it. The English still make barley water, flavoring it with lemon, as a nourishing drink. It is even sold in stores as a soft drink. There are two things you must do today if you are to have this soup tomorrow.

Soak overnight:
**1/2 cup barley in
    4 cups water**

Cook in pressure cooker at 15 pounds for 30 minutes, or simmer in covered kettle for several hours:
**2 oxtails
4 cups water**

When cool, strain broth and skim off fat. Remove meat from bones, chop fine and return meat to broth. Refrigerate overnight. Next day, skim off fat. Cook soaked barley in pressure cooker at 15 pounds for 15 minutes, or simmer until tender in covered pot.

Cook for 10 minutes in pressure cooker without cap, or in covered kettle:
**4 cups water
3/4 cup onions, minced
1 small carrot, minced
1 stalk celery, minced
2 cloves garlic, minced
1 bay leaf** (discard when cooked)
**3 tablespoons beef extract,
    salty type**

Add the cooked barley and the oxtail and broth. Return to stove and reheat gently for at least 20 minutes, being careful not to scorch as the barley settles to the bottom and, since it is a starch, tends to stick.

(Any leftover soup can be reheated or can be frozen satisfactorily.)

Serves 10

White Fish Soup
with Dill Dumplings

Sometimes at the fish market you cannot find just the type of fish you are accustomed to buying. Here is a recipe which will take whatever kind of white fish you find on hand, just so it is fish that will flake, such as ocean bass.

Grind together:
4 sprigs each tarragon, borage, basil or
   1 teaspoon fish herb blend
2 teaspoons herb salt

Bring to boil in 12 cups water and cook for 5 minutes:
2 pounds white fish
4 vegetable bouillon cubes
ground herb mixture

To make dumpling dough, mix together thoroughly:
2 cups all–purpose flour, sifted
1/2 teaspoon salt
4 teaspoons Royal baking powder (*do not use any other type, as the "double-acting" does not rise until acted on by oven heat*)
1 tablespoon fresh dill weed, chopped (*dry dill may be used but is not as good*)

Add and rub together by hand until mixture feels like coarse corn meal:
   1/4 cup vegetable shortening

(You may wish to substitute butter for this, because it gives a better flavor. If so, use 3/8 cup of butter. However the vegetable oil makes a lighter dumpling.)

In a measuring cup, beat:
1 egg

Add:
milk (*to make 3/4 cup liquid*)

Have egg and milk mixture at room temperature. Make a hole in the dry mixture to the bottom of the mixing bowl, so that when egg mixture is added it will go to the bottom. Mix quickly, just enough to incorporate ingredients. Do not overmix. Using a spoon and rubber scraper, dip the spoon in the hot soup; then take a small amount of dough and with the scraper push it off into the boiling soup. Keep doing this quickly until the top of the kettle of soup is covered with dumplings. (*They will quickly rise to the top as you drop them in.*) Cover the kettle immediately and cook for a few minutes until the dumplings are done. They should be moist on the outside and soft but not doughy on the inside. Serve.

Garnish each bowl with:
sprig of fresh dill

Serves 8

Watercress & Sorrel Soup

Wash thoroughly and remove all tough stems from spinach, French sorrel and watercress. Use only fresh herbs; dried ones will not do.

Simmer for 5 minutes in large, deep cooking pot (*do not brown*):
1/4 pound butter
1/2 leek, white part only, chopped fine

Add and boil for 10 minutes:
3 cups water
4 potatoes, peeled and quartered

Add and simmer gently for 45 minutes:
1/2 cup French sorrel, chopped
1 head lettuce, diced
1 cup spinach, chopped
1 teaspoon marjoram, chopped
1/2 teaspoon basil, chopped
2 teaspoons salt
5 cups boiling water

When finished simmering, put the vegetables through the blender in several small batches so they will not blow out of the top of the blender because of the heat. With the last batch, include and blend only slightly:
1/2 bunch fresh watercress, tops only

Reserve some sprigs of watercress for garnishing.

Reheat soup to serving temperature and garnish each bowl with:
sprig of watercress
sprinkle of paprika

Serves 8

Curried Mushroom Soup

This recipe was given to me originally by Torre Taggart when she was helping me with the cooking in the early days of the Ranch House. At that time we used canned mushroom soup, but this recipe, which has been altered by changes and additions, calls for fresh mushrooms, which are immeasurably better.

Make a massala by cooking slowly over low heat until clear:
4 tablespoons butter
1 onion, minced very fine
1 clove garlic, minced very fine

Add and mix well:
2 teaspoons curry powder

Simmer the massala for at least 5 to 10 minutes on very low heat; then add and blend in well:
**8 ounces mushrooms,
    chopped fine**
**5 vegetable or chicken
    bouillon cubes**

Cook about 5 minutes until mushrooms are done, then add and mix in well:
8 tablespoons flour

Add, cook and stir until thick:
8 cups milk

Stir in, mixing well:
2 tablespoons lemon juice
**3 tablespoons apricot jam
    or currant jelly**
1 tablespoon sherry
**peel of 1/2 lemon, chopped
    very fine**

Keep warm for about 30 minutes to blend flavors. Serve, garnished with:
**very thin slices of lemon
    or lime**

Serves 8

Onion-Cheddar Soup

In a heavy pot, simmer until
golden brown:
4 onions, sliced coarse
6 tablespoons butter

Add:
4 cups hot water

Mix in a blender; then add to
onions:
2 cups hot water
10 ounces aged Cheddar
  cheese, grated

Add to mixture:
1/2 cup Kikkoman soy sauce

Heat to serving temperature.

Garnish with:
chopped pimentos

(If there is any soup left over, it makes
an excellent base for other soups, or you
can add leftovers, such as rice or millet
or even diced potatoes.)

Serves 6 to 8

Chinese Peas

Prepare preceding recipe for
Onion–Cheddar Soup.

Wash and cut stems from:
1 pound Chinese peas,
  lightly cooked

Be sure to select only small, tender
peas; the large ones may have tough
fibers at the sides. When the broth
is done, add the peas, cover and cook
only enough to make them tender.
(They cook quickly as you will discover
if you have not cooked them before.)
Serve in individual ramekins.

You can make a delicious main
luncheon dish by increasing
the quantity of the broth and
adding cooked rice with the peas.
Serve in large soup bowls, along
with a melon salad.

Serves 4

Carnival in Basel

In Basel, Switzerland, the pre-Lenten carnival is opened on the Monday preceding Ash Wednesday with a traditional pre-dawn breakfast of flour soup and cheese. At 4 a.m. there is a sounding of drums and flutes, and the people come from all directions into town where the restaurants have prepared this special breakfast. At 5 a.m. they go to work so that they can quit at noon to begin their carnival festivities. There follow three days of drinking beer and dancing in the streets. I was served this soup by our Swiss friends Curt and Simone Walther. Here is her recipe. The Cheese Pie recipe is on page 105.

Flour Soup

Brown in a large frying pan, stirring constantly, over low heat to prevent scorching:
1 cup white flour

When nicely brown add and mix well:
4 tablespoons butter

Add to desired thickness, stirring with a wire whisk:
8 cups chicken broth
pinch basil
pinch marjoram

Adjust flavor with:
salt to taste

Bring ingredients to a good boil and cook for about 5 minutes very slowly. Serve in large soup bowls with a good sprinkling of:
aged Emmentaler cheese
grated parsley, chopped fine

Serves 8

*Dancing in
the streets.*

Fresh Salmon Chowder

Salmon collars are the neck portion of the fresh salmon that are cut off when the fish is cut into steaks. Ask your fish market to reserve these for you, or the small pieces left when the steaks are cut. Of course the steaks themselves can be used, if you can afford the extravagance. This is one of the finest dishes that can be made from fresh salmon.

Boil until just done, don't overcook:
2 pounds salmon
1 cup water

Drain, skim and reserve liquid. Remove bones, skin and dark parts from fish.

Fry until clear (*do not brown*):
1 small onion, chopped fine
2 tablespoons butter

Parboil for 5 minutes in enough water to cover:
2 cups potatoes, peeled
    and cut into 1/2–inch cubes

Drain and add potatoes and fish liquid to cooked onions.
Grind in mortar:
1 teaspoon salt
1 teaspoon herb salt
1/8 teaspoon fish herb blend
1/8 teaspoon white pepper

Add herb mixture to potato and onion mixture, cook for 5 minutes, cover and simmer about 10 minutes; then add:
1 cup coffee cream
1 cup scalded milk
5 soda crackers (*soaked in
    a little of the milk*)
2 tablespoons butter
the cooked salmon

Do not boil, but serve very hot. Too much heating may curdle the soup. If this happens, drain off liquid and put it through blender; then mix with solids and reheat.

Serves 6

Clam Chowder,
New England Style

Mix together in a saucepan:
3 tablespoons butter
5 tablespoons flour

Add and cook until thickened:
4 cups milk
1 13–ounce can evaporated milk
13 ounces water

Remove rind, cut into small
cubes and fry until crisp but not
too brown:
1 ounce salt pork

Remove pork from fat and reserve.
Add to pork fat and cook until clear:
1 small onion, chopped fine

Peel, dice and cook in 1/2 cup water
until done but not mushy:
2 small potatoes

Mix all ingredients together and
add as seasoning:
1 1/2 teaspoons herb salt
pinch caraway seeds
1 tablespoon sherry

Adjust seasoning with:
salt to taste
a dash of white pepper

Add and stir in:
1 1/2 pints minced clams
 and juice

Heat in double boiler to serving
temperature, no hotter, as it
tends to curdle after clams have
been added.

Garnish with:
chopped parsley
paprika

Serves 8

Spiced Vegetable & Tomato Soup

Grind together in a blender the following seeds and spices:
2 teaspoons coriander
1/4 teaspoon ground
cardamom seeds
1 teaspoon turmeric
1/2 teaspoon cumin
1/2 teaspoon peppercorns
1/2 teaspoon poppy seeds
1/2 teaspoon celery seeds

In a saucepan sauté the green onions until clear and then add the seed and spice mixture from above:
2 tablespoons butter
1 bunch green onions,
chopped fine

Steam the following in a pressure cooker until tender, but not mushy:
2 cups celery, chopped fine
2 carrots, chopped fine
1 bunch radishes,
chopped fine
2 bay leaves
1/2 teaspoon dried basil

Combine all of the above ingredients and add:
2 46–ounce cans Campbell's
tomato soup *(diluted with*
the usual amount of water)

Heat and serve with:
chopped parsley

*The cooking must
be well done.*

Tomato Soup
with Cloven Hoof

Boil for about 10 minutes:
8 medium–sized tomatoes,
**   unpeeled, cut up**
2 cups water

While still hot, put into muslin cloth and hang to drain as you would in making jelly.

Add to drained juice:
1 teaspoon sugar for each
**   cup of juice**
powdered cloves (*only as much*
*   as can be picked up on the point of a*
*   paring knife. Use caution! Too much*
*   will overpower the tomato flavor.*
*   You can always add more, but you*
*   can't take it out once it is in.*)
salt to taste
red coloring, 1 drop

Subtleness is the secret of this wonderful soup. If you get the proper proportions it will delight you. Tomatoes vary in flavor so you must be gentle with the cloves each time you make it, bringing all of your gourmet artistry to bear in concocting this seemingly simple recipe. It should be a clear, bright broth, not sharp, perfectly blended.

For interest, add:
alphabet noodles
    (*a few to each serving*)

Or, as the Japanese do with their soups, add to each serving:
1 thin slice of fresh mushroom
a tiny slice of green pepper
the thinnest slice of celery

Serve hot or chilled.

Serves 4

Fordhook Lima Bean
& Ham Soup

Soak overnight:
**1 cup large dry limas
in 6 cups water**

Next day, using soaking water, cook beans slowly in covered pot until done, or at 15 pounds pressure for 15 minutes in pressure cooker, with:
1 pound ham shank

When done, discard fat and ham bone, chop ham fine and reserve it. Skim fat from liquid, put beans and liquid through blender, then add chopped ham.

Cook in covered pan for 10 minutes, or in pressure cooker for 1 minute at 15 pounds pressure:
**1 cup water
1 clove garlic, minced
1 large onion, minced
1 stalk celery, minced
1 small green pepper, minced
2 1/4 teaspoons soup herb blend
1 1/4 teaspoons herb salt
6 soup bouillon cubes,
    chicken or vegetable**

Add vegetables to broth, reheat to serving temperature. For an unusual garnish, make small balls of:
cream cheese

Roll cheese balls in:
chopped parsley

Drop into each bowl of hot soup.

Serves 6

Belgian Beef Soup

Brown well in heavy skillet:
**1 1/2 pounds beef cross ribs,
cut in 4–inch pieces**
(*add no fat; there is enough
on the meat*)

Add to meat and cook until done:
**4 cups water
1 small onion, minced
1 bay leaf** (*discard when cooked*)
**1 1/2 teaspoons soup herb blend
1 1/2 teaspoons herb salt**

Cool, lift out meat, discard bones and chop meat fine. Skim broth well (*or better, refrigerate overnight and take off fat*).

Mix together and cook for 10 minutes, or in pressure cooker at 15 pounds for 1 minute:
**1/2 onion, sliced very thin
1 small stalk celery, sliced thin
2 fresh string beans, sliced thin
1/2 green pepper, chopped fine
1 carrot, chopped fine
2 tablespoons lemon juice
2 cups water
6 beef bouillon cubes
broth from cross ribs**

When done, add:
chopped beef

If a heavier soup is desired, fine noodles may be boiled separately and added.

Serves 6

Mulligatawny

This is an East Indian curried soup and a quite unusual, flavorful combination of ingredients.

Fry slowly for at least 5 minutes, so it will brown without burning:
1 cup carrots, chopped fine
1 cup green peppers, cut fine
1 cup tart green apples, cut fine
1 cup onion, chopped fine in
    4 tablespoons butter
    (clarified butter called ghee is best)

Add and continue to cook slowly until flour browns:
2 teaspoons flour

Mix together, add and boil for about 2 minutes:
8 cups chicken or beef broth
1 1/2 teaspoons curry powder
1 teaspoon salt
2 teaspoons chicken or beef base
1 cup yogurt, stirred well
1/4 teaspoon cardamom
    seed, powdered
2 tablespoons tomato paste
2 teaspoons sugar
2 1/2 teaspoons lemon juice

Add to finished soup:
1 cup cooked rice

Garnish with:
a sprinkling of fresh, finely
    grated coconut, or a
    paper-thin slice of lemon

Serves 8

I returned from living in India.

Tortilla Soup

Sauté until clear:
2 onions, chopped fine
4 ounces butter
2 teaspoons garlic, minced

In a separate pan simmer until
tender, not mushy:
6 zucchini, coarsely chopped
2 quarts chicken broth

Then add:
3 vegetable bouillon cubes
10 corn tortillas

Combine all above ingredients
and blend until smooth adding:
salt to taste
hot sauce to desired zip

Serve hot with:
chopped tomatoes
sour cream
crushed tortilla chips

SALADS & DRESSINGS

It made quite a show.

We have grown as many as ten varieties of lettuce at the Ranch House. Here's the list:

Romaine, both red and green; Oak Leaf, red and green; Boston Butter; Kentucky Bibb (limestone); Black–Seeded Simpson; Salad Bowl; Prize Head Bronze; Chicory (or endive); Great Lakes; Iceberg Head.

So much time and attention had to be given to cultivation, and such an amount of good compost used, that we were unable to keep up the pace. So we have settled on a few favorites, as you undoubtedly have also, if you have it in your garden. It is at its prime when picked early in the morning when the water is still in it from the night's growth.

It is so important that the lettuce be fresh, and very crisp and dry when used in salads. If it is washed and stored in plastic bags in the refrigerator at about 40° F., it makes a wonderfully crunchy pick-up in salad to begin a meal.

I think it is important that the dressing be at room temperature. If it is too cold it will cling to the lettuce leaves, not dressing it but smothering it. The chilled lettuce will chill the dressing enough, especially if the bowl is cold also.

We use various types of lettuce for texture, flavor and color. The bronze varieties are wonderful for color, and what can equal the Boston Butter or Bibb lettuce for taste and texture? Limestone is the name currently used in good restaurants for this Kentucky Bibb variety.

A friend who is the society editor of a newspaper said, speaking of restaurant dining: "That ubiquitous baked potato – how I abhor it!"

I feel that way about the salads offered in most restaurants – the equally ubiquitous salad, with choice of dressing; the waitress asking, "Will you have French, Thousand Island or Roquefort dressing?" And after reading about all the lawsuits, we know that "Roquefort" really means Bleu cheese or a reasonable facsimile; that French dressing is too orange in color, much too tart, and not with the real sharpness that comes from a good wine vinegar, but from some kind of added acid; that Thousand Island is a composite of God-knows-what that was left in the kitchen the night before last. So, here we have tried to avoid the usual – and how far out we have gone you will have to decide for yourself when you make some of these things suggested. We like them; but then, we make them, and that may be the reason. However, our customers also like them and that is very important in a restaurant operation.

Crab Salad

For a wedding party of two hundred which we catered, the pièce de résistance was a huge man-eating clam shell filled with this salad. It made quite a show.

Mix together:
**1 pound crab meat, cooked
    and flaked
1 cup celery, chopped fine
1/2 green pepper, chopped fine
1/2 cup cucumber, peeled
    and chopped fine
1/2 cup green peas, cooked
    and chilled
1/2 cup baby lima beans,
    cooked and chilled
1 hard–boiled egg, sliced**

Add, sprinkling on as ingredients are mixed, so it will be evenly distributed:
1 1/2 teaspoons herb salt

Mix together and add:
**1 cup mayonnaise
1 teaspoon lemon or
    lime juice**

Line the bowl in which the salad is to be served with:
bronze lettuce leaves

Mound the crab mixture in the bowl and garnish with:
blueberries, fresh or frozen

Scatter the berries over the salad or make a design with them. Chill the salad for at least 4 hours before serving. It should be served very cold.

Serves 6

Green Bean &
Onion Salad

Cook until done but not mushy, then drain and chill in refrigerator:
1 pound slender green beans
> *(the wide, coarse beans are too tough for this salad)*

Peel and slice very thin:
2 large Spanish onions

Prepare a marinade, having all ingredients at room temperature:
1/2 cup lemon juice
1/2 cup wine vinegar
1/4 teaspoon each tarragon, basil, marjoram, thyme or
1 teaspoon salad herb blend
1 1/2 teaspoons herb salt

Add and mix well:
1 cup olive oil

Put 2/3 of the marinade over chilled and drained green beans, and 1/3 of it over the sliced onions. Let both stand 15 minutes, then drain.

Line salad plates with:
lettuce leaves

Arrange green beans on the lettuce, put a small mound of onion slices on them and garnish with:
thin strips of pimento
a few capers

Chill well on the plates before serving.

Serves 6

Cabbage Combination

Steam for 1 minute only, then drain and chill:
1/2 head of cabbage, cut in 1/2-inch cubes

When cabbage has chilled, mix it with:
2 cups celery, sliced thin
2 cups unpeeled apples, cut in 1/2-inch cubes
1 cup broken pecans

To make dressing, mix in blender:
1/2 pint sour cream
3 ounces Philadelphia cream cheese
1/2 teaspoon poppy seeds
dash turmeric
1/2 teaspoon salt
dash onion salt to taste

Combine cabbage mixture and dressing. For each serving, line salad plate with lettuce leaf. With ice-cream scoop, put a mound of salad on the lettuce.

Garnish generously with:
minced parsley

Pass a bowl of:
French dressing *(for those who want a variation in flavor)*

Serves 8 or more

Big Stinky Salad

Here's something great to serve with barbecued steaks or a beef roast, in place of the usual tossed green salad. Once you bring yourself to concocting the Big Stinky, you'll repeat it many times. It's best when broccoli and other vegetables are first in season, with small and tender stalks.

Put into the freezer so that it will be frozen when you are ready to use it:
1/4 pound Danish blue cheese

For each 4 servings steam only until tender, then drain and chill:
2 large heads broccoli, cut up
1 small head cauliflower, cut up
4 Brussels sprouts
8 asparagus spears

To make dressing, mix together:
1/2 pint sour cream
1/4 cup French capers
1 teaspoon salad herb blend
1/2 teaspoon onion salt
1/4 teaspoon garlic salt

For each serving line salad plate with:
lettuce leaf

Arrange chilled vegetables on lettuce. Spoon over them some of the dressing in a way to enhance the arrangement, not cover it up. With a sharp knife shave off a generous amount of the frozen blue cheese onto each portion. The freezing makes it easy to handle this sticky cheese.

Garnish generously with:
minced parsley

The parsley is the only garnish needed as the salad is supposed to be green and greenish white in color.

Serves 4

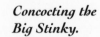

Concocting the Big Stinky.

Deviled Shrimp Salad

Mix well together:
2 red onions, thinly sliced
1 cup pitted black olives
4 tablespoons chopped
      pimentos
1 cup lemon juice
1/2 cup olive oil
2 tablespoons wine vinegar
2 cloves garlic, minced
1 bay leaf
2 tablespoons dry mustard
1/2 teaspoon salt
pinch black pepper
2 lemons, thinly sliced

Add and mix in:
5 pounds of prepared shrimp

Serves 12

Fresh Fruit with Pomegranate Dressing

Line salad plate with:
bronze lettuce leaf

Arrange on lettuce:
fresh fruit slices

Whip in mixer at high speed:
1/2 pint sour cream
4 ounces Philadelphia
      cream cheese
1/4 cup pomegranate
      sauce (*page 39*)**, or**
      1/4 cup Grenadine syrup

For texture, sprinkle on:
fresh coconut
pomegranate seeds (*optional*)

Dressing serves 8

Fresh Fruit with Cardamom Sauce

If you are not familiar with this spice, here is a sauce recipe that will demonstrate its wonderful flavor. On fresh fruit, it will offer a happy taste experience.

Simmer over low heat for 2 minutes to blend flavors:
1/2 cup water
1/2 cup orange blossom honey
1/4 teaspoon cardamom seed, powdered
6 large mint leaves, chopped
   (dried mint will not do)
1/4 teaspoon salt

Cool to room temperature, then add and stir in well:
1/2 cup good port wine
1/8 cup Benedictine

Peel and slice enough for 8 servings:
melon, all kinds
avocados
apples
oranges

Arrange fruit attractively on salad plates lined with:
red lettuce leaves

Garnish plates of fruit with:
parsley
pitted black cherries

Serves 8

Javanese Salad

Mix together:
1/2 teaspoon cream of tartar
2 cups cold water

Peel, then dip immediately into cream of tartar solution:
4 bananas

This will keep the bananas from turning dark. Drain them well for at least 30 minutes.

Chop fine and spread on foil or a plate:
1 cup peanuts or blanched almonds

Roll the bananas in the nuts. The bananas will be very sticky and can be nicely coated with the nuts.

Prepare:
1 avocado, peeled and sliced
1 papaya, peeled and sliced
1 mango, peeled and sliced
   (optional)
pineapple slices, fresh or canned

Hawaiian Salad

Mix together:
1 cup mayonnaise
1/2 cup lime marmalade
2 tablespoons crème de menthe
   (or less, according to taste)

Line 4 salad plates with:
lettuce leaves

Lay the coated banana on the lettuce leaf, arrange the sliced fruit around it in an attractive pattern, and spoon on some of the dressing.

In Java, you would put fresh flowers on the table and scatter a few of their petals on each salad plate.

A friend, Vivienne Moody, brought back from her trip to Hawaii some excellent salad dressing. We tried, and I think we succeeded, to duplicate it using papaya seeds. The following method is very simple but excellent. I hope you like it as much as we do.

Make the following dressing.

Put into blender:
32 ounces peanut oil
4 ounces honey
3 lemons, juice
1 medium onion, peeled
1 teaspoon onion salt
8 ounces vinegar
seeds from 2 papayas

Place soft lettuce (*like butter type*) on a plate. Chop some other lettuce leaves and put them in the middle of the plate. Lay some slices of papaya on the chopped leaves. Spoon some of the dressing over the salad and then sprinkle some freshly grated coconut on top. Serve very cold.

Pesto Chicken Salad

Roast and bone and cut into
large bite–size pieces:
6 whole roasting chickens

Soak in boiling water for 3 to 5
minutes, drain, and cut into slivers:
3 ounces sun dried tomatoes

Toast in a 350° oven for 10 to 15
minutes, just until they begin
to brown:
1 cup pine nuts

Toss all above ingredients gently
together (*including chicken*) with:
**2 medium red onions,
    slivered or minced
2 red or yellow bell peppers,
    very thin strips or minced
6 celery ribs, diced small**

Fold in the following
pesto mayonnaise.

Mix together:
**1 cup pesto sauce
1 1/2 cups mayonnaise**

Serves 12

Tarragon Chicken Salad with Wild Rice & Asparagus

Roast and bone and cut into large
bite–size pieces:
3 whole roasting chickens

Steam asparagus until crisp–tender,
then run immediately under very
cold water to retain color. Cut into
pieces about 1 inch long:
1 1/2 pounds fresh asparagus

Gently mix and combine with
chicken and asparagus:
**2 cups cooked wild rice
2 bunches green onions, minced**

Fold the following dressing into
above mixture and, preferably, let
it marinate for a least 1 hour before
serving.

Combine in blender:
**1 1/2 cups olive oil
3/4 cup white wine vinegar
3 large cloves garlic
1 bunch fresh tarragon
1/4 cup Dijon mustard
3 sprigs fresh basil
salt and pepper to taste**

Chinese Chicken Salad

Serve on dinner plate that has been chilled and lined with green or red leaf lettuce. Mound salad in center and surround with crackers and garnish vegetables.

Garnish with:
sliced tomatoes
asparagus stalks, steamed
   crisp–tender
sliced hot house cucumbers
Carr's table water crackers
   (*or equivalent*)

Serves 6

Whisk together:
1/4 cup Mirin saki wine
1/4 cup toasted sesame oil
1 cup peanut oil
2 1/2 ounces soy sauce
1/4 cup wine vinegar
1/4 cup sugar
1/4 teaspoon powdered ginger
2 teaspoons dry mustard

Prepare the chicken mixture
as follows:
2 cups cooked chicken
1/2 cup celery, cut up
1/2 cup green peppers, cut up
1/2 cup red sweet peppers,
   cut up
1/4 cup water chestnuts, sliced
1/4 cup Mung bean sprouts
   that have been wilted
   in hot water
1/2 cup above sauce
   (*or more if desired*)

Lay a bed of rice noodles (*cooked*) on serving plate. Spoon on chicken mixture. Lay around the edges of the noodles thin slices of pickles, ginger, pickled radishes (*red variety*), and some thinly sliced cucumbers.

Serves 4

Ranch House
Salad Dressing

Mix well together:
1 cup red wine vinegar
1/2 teaspoon dry mustard
**1/2 teaspoon fresh–ground
    black pepper**

Grind together and mix in:
4 sprigs basil
4 sprigs marjoram
2 sprigs tarragon
2 sprigs lemon thyme
2 sprigs rosemary
1 teaspoon herb salt
    *(use only fresh herbs;
    dry will not do)*

Add and mix in:
2 cups olive oil

Do not refrigerate.

Sesame Seed Dressing

*Ground-up sesame seeds, sometimes called
tahini, are available in specialty food
shops. Like peanut butter, oil comes to the
top and it has to be mixed before using.
It is often eaten as a spread on dark bread,
and it makes a delicious salad dressing.*

Mix together:
**1/2 cup sesame seed butter,
    thinned with a very small
    amount of boiling water**
lemon juice to taste

To give it a salty flavor you
may add:
Kikkoman soy sauce to taste

Samoa Salad Dressing

This delicious dressing is good on fresh fruit salads or desserts. You will need ginger marmalade that is made without lemon juice. There is a brand that comes from Ledbury, England, named after the town.

Put in mixer and whip until smooth:
1/2 pint sour cream
1/4 cup ginger marmalade
    (without lemon juice)
pinch of curry powder

For texture, sprinkle on:
raw, unsalted pignolia nuts

As a variation, instead of the curry powder add:
2 leaves pennyroyal,
    chopped

More marmalade may be used for stronger flavor, if desired.

Swordfish Salad Dressing

Combine all ingredients well and toss with baby assorted greens:
12 ounces walnut oil
4 ounces lime juice
1 1/2 tablespoons
    fresh dill weed, minced
1 teaspoon salt
2 tablespoons garlic, minced
1/8 teaspoon cayenne pepper

Serve with strips of chilled grilled swordfish and garnish with sliced sweet red onions, avocado wedges, and smoked scallops.

Almond Maple Dressing

Whip together:
**1 pound almond butter,
    coarse grind**
**10 ounces coconut–pineapple
    juice**
4 ounces maple syrup
**1/4 teaspoon ground
    cardamom seed**
**1 tablespoon lemon
    or lime juice**

Wait until all ingredients are
thoroughly mixed.

Serve over fresh fruit salad.

CHEESE

*I met him at
the Ranch House.*

A young bride (nameless, naturally!) invited us one evening for dinner. She was trying out a new dish – Swiss cheese fondue.

We gathered at the table with, I am sure, mixed emotions, and our not-yet-experienced hostess timidly lifted the lid from a large casserole. We found ourselves gazing at a strange yellowish blob of something sitting in the middle of a little lake of lighter colored liquid. Bravely, we prodded the resisting blob with chunks of bread made soggy by the liquid, and gave up, finding the mess inedible.

No tears were shed — these were her friends — and we ate our salad amidst laughter and analysis of the mishap. I asked if she had used aged cheese, and she hardly knew what I meant. The recipe had not specified, and so . . .

I am not an authority on cheese but am able to make some comments out of a little experience with it. It is common knowledge, of course, that cheese varies widely with the country or area producing it. Some European cheeses are so perishable they cannot be shipped from their place of origin. There are myriad varieties, both domestic and foreign. Each cook must choose favorites among the many classifications, then look for qualities of flavor and texture within each class.

On the Swiss Independence day I attended a dinner that had as its feature one hundred varieties of cheese that had been sent from all over Europe. What a feast! New, green cheese will not melt but turns into a sort of soft stringy gum. Aging somehow affects the cheese so that it will melt. As much as a year is required to age good cheese properly. To make green cheese more soluble, and perhaps to dilute the more expensive aged cheese, it is "processed" by the addition of gums, water, powdered milk, and so on; it lacks the quality and rich flavor of aged cheese. The cheese used in Welsh rarebit and in fondues should always be aged. A simple way to tell whether or not cheese is aged is to break it. Aged cheese will crumble easily; green cheese will not.

Hungarian Noodles & Cottage Cheese

Cook together until just done but not mushy:
1/4 cup butter
1 cup onions, sliced thin
1 clove garlic, minced

Mix together and add:
1 pound creamed cottage cheese
1 pound sour cream
1 teaspoon herb salt

The cottage cheese and sour cream coming from the refrigerator will have cooled down the mixture.

Add:
**1 pound noodles, cooked
   and drained**

Mix well together and then warm again until just hot enough to serve. Too much heating will make the cheese stringy and objectionable.

Serves 6

Nut & Cheese Vegetable Loaf

Sauté just until soft:
2 tablespoons oil
2 cloves garlic, minced
1 pound mushrooms, sliced

Cook until a little dry:
2 tablespoons oil
2 green peppers, griced
3 zucchini, griced

Add and cook, about 1 minute:
1 ear corn, cut from cob

Stir in:
1 pound Cheddar cheese, griced
**3 slices whole wheat bread,
   crumbled in blender**
1 cup cashew pieces
1/4 cup sunflower seeds, hulled

Add and stir in after beating together:
6 eggs
1/2 cup cream
1 1/2 teaspoons herb salt
1 teaspoon vegetable herb blend
1/2 teaspoon ground pepper

Make into 2 loaves in greased loaf pan. Bake until done and knife comes out clean, at 350° for about 45 minutes. Loaf should be firm and may need to be baked at least 1 hour or more.

Serves 8

Stuffed Ravioli

Prepare pasta for ravioli squares.
Mix together the following:
1 carton Ricotta cheese
  (16-ounce size)
1/2 cup Italian parsley,
  chopped fine
1/2 cup toasted walnut pieces
2 cups grated Parmesan cheese
2 egg yolks

Stuff ravioli pockets and place on
top layer, sealing the edges with a
little water.

To prepare:
Drop into boiling water for just a
few minutes, no longer or they tend
to come apart. Serve with a light
tomato sauce.

Serves 6

European Quiche

Line a 9–inch glass pie plate with
good crust. Spread over crust:
sliced, toasted almonds

Mix together:
5 beaten eggs
1 tablespoon flour
2 1/2 cups warm light cream
1 teaspoon herb salt
dash nutmeg
dash cayenne

Cut 6 slices Provolone cheese into
strips and lay them on the almonds
in the crust. Pour over this the egg
mixture and bake at 350° for 1 hour
until knife comes out clean.

A variant:

Braise 1 or 1 1/2 cups sliced
mushrooms in butter, spread them
over the almonds and cheese, and
bake as above.

Serves 6

Spinach Soufflé

Heat in pan:
3 tablespoons butter
3 tablespoons flour

When melted and combined,
add and cook until thick:
1 cup milk
1/2 cup cooked spinach,
  drained and chopped
1 pimento, chopped *(optional)*
1/2 teaspoon herb salt

When cool, add and stir in well:
6 egg yolks

Beat until stiff:
6 egg whites
1/2 teaspoon salt

Mix 1/3 of whites into spinach
mixture, folding in. Turn this mixture
into the rest of the whites and fold
in gently. Bake in ungreased dish for
45 minutes at 350º, or until knife
comes out clean.

Serve with cheese sauce *(page 172)*.

Serves 4

Cheese Pie

Line a shallow, round 9–inch
pan with:
rich pastry crust

Crimp edges so they will hold up,
making it easy to remove the pieces
when baked.

Mix together the following
ingredients:
1 1/2 cups milk *(or part cream*
  for extra richness)
3 eggs, beaten
1/2 teaspoon salt
1/4 teaspoon white pepper

Line pastry shell with:
aged Emmentaler cheese,
  sliced thin

Pour in egg and milk mixture.
Bake at 350º for about 40 minutes
until the custard is set. Many
variations of this pie have been
invented but the original is this very
simple and very good quiche from
Alsace Lorraine. Often these pies are
made in smaller sizes, about 3 to 4
inches, but the large ones are better
because they don't dry out so much
in the baking.

Serves 6

Fondue Gruyère

Whenever we visit Switzerland we go to the Chateau Gruyère where that famous cheese was first made. In the little village they make the traditional fondue which is supposed to have originated there, and they taught me how to make it. Here is the original recipe: there are variations, but this is how it was prepared and served to us.

Heat in a pottery fondue dish which has been rubbed with garlic cloves:
1 1/2 cups dry white wine

Grate and mix together:
1/2 pound aged Gruyère cheese
1/2 pound aged Emmentaler cheese

Add the grated cheese to the heated wine and stir until it begins to dissolve. As you stir it may seem to be making a sticky ball. Do not despair! All will be well. Sieve and stir in, to bring the cheese and wine together to a good smooth consistency:
3 tablespoons potato starch
   (*no other starch will work; do not first dissolve in water*)

Keep stirring and add:
2 or 3 tablespoons Kirsch
   (*cherry brandy, also called Kirschwasser*)
dash nutmeg (*optional*)

When the mixture is smooth and begins to thicken slightly, take the casserole to the table and place over a small alcohol stove.

At Gruyère each guest is provided with a long two–tined fork with a wooden handle. A large wooden bowl, placed within everybody's reach, is filled with chunks of sourdough or French bread.

With your fork spear a piece of bread and dip it into the fondue, turning it to catch the drip as you lift it out. Anyone who drops a piece of bread into the fondue is kissed by the girl next to him. At the last there forms on the bottom of the casserole a browned crust which everyone fights for.

Serves 6

EGGS

Touch no eggs,
use no sugar,
eat no fat.

THOSE WONDERFUL GLOBULETS OF DELIGHT

CALLED EGGS HARDLY NEED ANYTHING SAID ABOUT THEM.

HERE ARE A FEW THINGS YOU MAY NOT HAVE THOUGHT OF,

ESPECIALLY IF YOU ARE A YOUNGER, LESS EXPERIENCED COOK.

THE WHITES OF EGGS HAVE VERY LITTLE FLAVOR.

THEIR MISSION IN COOKERY IS TO BIND THINGS TOGETHER

OR LIGHTLY HOLD OTHER INGREDIENTS. THEIR MAIN VALUE,

THEN, IS THEIR VISCOSITY, THEIR STICK–TOGETHERNESS. THIS

CAPACITY IS ENHANCED, WHEN THEY ARE BEING BEATEN, BY

THE ADDITION OF SMALL AMOUNTS OF SALT OR SUGAR (NEVER

FLOUR OR ANYTHING OF THAT DRY NATURE WHICH HAS TO

BE RECONSTITUTED). EVEN A TINY DROP OF ANY OIL, OR A BIT OF THE YOLK WITH ITS HIGH OIL CONTENT, MAY PREVENT THEIR BEING WHIPPED SATISFACTORILY.

WHEN A RECIPE CALLS FOR WHIPPING BOTH THE YOLKS AND WHITES, I ADD THE SALT OF THE RECIPE EQUALLY TO EACH AND WHIP THE YOLKS FIRST. YOLKS HAVE A MUCH HEAVIER BODY AND SO HOLD UP LONGER, AND IT TAKES LONGER TO WHIP THEM. THEY SHOULD BE BEATEN UNTIL THEY ARE LEMON COLORED.

THE WHITES WHIP IN LESS TIME AND WILL NOT HOLD UP VERY LONG, SO THEY SHOULD BE WHIPPED JUST BEFORE THEY ARE TO BE FOLDED IN. A FOLDING MOTION SHOULD ALWAYS BE USED TO INCORPORATE EVEN MORE AIR IN THEM AND THUS COUNTERACT THE LOSS OF AIR DURING THE MIXING PROCESS. THE YOLKS HAVE LESS LIGHTNESS, YET HAVE MOST OF THE FLAVOR THAT IS IN THE EGG, AND ADD RICHNESS TO EVERYTHING CONTAINING THEM.

EGGS ARE A MULTIPURPOSE FOOD, USED ON THEIR OWN OR IN COMBINATIONS OR TO AID IN THE STRUCTURE OF SOME MORE COMPLICATED DISH. IF COOKED ALONE IN VARIOUS WAYS, A LITTLE SPRINKLING OF A DELICATE HERB MIXTURE AND SALT GROUND TOGETHER — A MERE SUGGESTION OF AN HERB BLEND — IS WONDERFUL. COMBINED WITH OTHER THINGS, SUCH AS VEGETABLES OR MUSHROOMS, THE TRADITIONAL BOUQUET IS EXCELLENT. IF THEY LOSE THEIR IDENTITY AS THEY BIND THINGS TOGETHER IN OTHER DISHES, THE HERBS USED WILL BE THOSE THAT COMPLEMENT THE MAIN INGREDIENTS.

Egg Foo Yung

Wash and chop:
1 cup parsley
**1/2 cup green onions, tops
    and bottoms, cut fine**
**1 large green pepper, cut in
    long fine strips**
1 bunch watercress tops (optional)
1/2 cup celery tops
**1 cup water chestnuts,
    sliced rather thick**
**1/2 cup boiled ham or
    chicken, sliced thin** (optional)
**1/2 cup bamboo shoots,
    sliced thin**
**1/2 pound fresh bean
    sprouts**

Beat separately:
**8 egg yolks with
    1/2 teaspoon salt**
**8 egg whites with
    1/2 teaspoon salt**

Fold yolks into whites.

Add from sifter:
8 tablespoons flour

Fold in gently, with only enough strokes to incorporate completely. Fold egg mixture into chopped vegetables.

Heat peanut oil in large skillet or deep griddle so that batter dropped in will sizzle around edges. Drop in a large tablespoon of batter for each cake. Spoon oil over cakes to seal them. Turn with large spatula aided by spoon, flipping gently. Brown on both sides. If this is done correctly there will be no splashing of the batter at the edges of the cakes. Don't worry about the vegetables getting done; they will cook just enough if the oil is the right temperature.

Serve with the following sauce spooned over the cakes.

Put in saucepan:
1 quart water
1 vegetable bouillon cube
4 tablespoons soy sauce

Thicken with:
**6 tablespoons cornstarch,
    dissolved in water** (no flour,
    as this is a clear sauce)

Put 3 cakes on each plate, lapping one over the other, and spoon over them the hot sauce mixture. Serve with rice.

Serves 8

Curried Stuffed Eggs

Boil gently for 10 minutes, starting in cold water; do not let eggs roll in the boiling water:
12 eggs

Cool eggs, dipping them in cold water to make them easy to handle, peel off the shells and cut the eggs across. Gently remove the yolks without damaging the whites. Reserve whites and yolks.

Fry gently until onions are clear:
1 clove garlic, minced
1 small onion, minced, in
  2 tablespoons butter

Add and continue to cook for 5 minutes over low heat:
2 tablespoons curry powder
few drops lemon juice

Mash egg yolks and mix into the curry, then press this mixture into the egg–white halves. Put the filled halves together and secure them with toothpicks; lay them in a casserole.

Heat together:
4 tablespoons butter
4 tablespoons flour

Add and cook, stirring constantly with wire whisk until thick:
2 cups milk
1/2 cup coffee cream
1 bay leaf (*discard when cooked*)
1/2 teaspoon herb salt
  or regular salt
1 tablespoon sherry

Pour sauce over eggs in casserole, reheat to serving temperature and serve, accompanied by rice. Remove toothpicks gently as eggs are spooned out on plate, so that the eggs will not come apart.

Serves 6 to 8

Quiche Lorraine (Swiss)

Line glass pie pan with:
rich pie crust (*page 268*)
   (*make it thin*)

Fry until very crisp, then drain
on paper towel:
8 slices bacon, cut thick

Put in blender:
4 eggs
1 tablespoon flour
1/2 teaspoon salt
2 cups cream (*a little heavier
   than coffee cream*)
dash nutmeg
**1/2 teaspoon Worcestershire
   sauce**
dash of cognac (*optional*)

Blend only until mixed. Do not
overblend or custard will not
set right.

Crumble bacon slices in pie crust;
cover with thin slices of:
aged Swiss cheese

Add egg mixture and bake at 350°
until custard sets, about 45 minutes.

Serves 6

Eggs Dijonnaise

Mix the following ingredients together in a saucepan and simmer over low heat for 10 minutes:

4 ounces Dijon mustard
8 ounces heavy cream
2 ounces lemon juice
12 ounces white wine
12 green onions, minced
8 tablespoons tarragon
12 ounces sweet butter
1 1/2 teaspoons salt
1/2 teaspoon white pepper

When done, remove from heat and add:
2 cups Béchamel sauce
    (page 43)

Butter the inside of individual casseroles and line with cooked spinach. Add 2 eggs to each casserole and bake at 400° just until whites are set. Pour above sauce over eggs and serve.

Serves 8

VEGETABLES

We ate only vegetables.

Some people dislike the term "vegetarian" very much. They frequently mention that they eat cheese, eggs and other dairy products, which surely are not vegetables firsthand, but filtered through the cows and chickens!

Protein, found to be so essential nutritionally, must not be neglected in the diet of those who eat no meat. I have tried to put most of these entrees together so that dietary requirements will not be neglected. Some of the dishes are higher in protein, minerals and vitamins than meat. Many types of nuts, seeds, cheese, grains and milk products are used.

"I SELDOM EAT VEGETABLES, BUT HERE I FIND MYSELF EATING THEM FIRST!" THIS REMARK IS OFTEN MADE BY PEOPLE WHO DINE WITH US. THERE IS NO SPECIAL MAGIC IN OUR METHODS, EXCEPT THAT WE MAKE CERTAIN THAT THE VEGETABLES WE USE ARE FRESH, AND WE DO NOT OVERCOOK THEM. THEN WE SERVE THEM WITH A SAUCE THAT DOES NOT COVER UP THE FLAVOR, BUT ONLY ENHANCES IT. VEGETABLES MORE THAN 24 HOURS OLD, NOT REFRIGERATED OR PRESERVED IN SOME MANNER, HAVE LOST 90 PERCENT OF THEIR FOOD VALUE, SAY AUTHORITIES ON NUTRITION. THE NATURAL SUGAR CONTENT OF THE VEGETABLE IS WHAT GIVES IT ITS DELICIOUS FLAVOR AND WHEN ITS FRESHNESS IS LOST, THIS SUGAR TURNS TO STARCH. SO, WHEN FRESHNESS IS LOST PRACTICALLY ALL IS LOST, BOTH FLAVOR AND NUTRITION.

THE BEST WAY TO PRESERVE THE PRECIOUS SUGAR IN COOKED VEGETABLES IS TO SEE THAT THE COOKING TIME IS SHORT, SO THAT IT DOES NOT BLEED OUT INTO THE WATER OR GET DRIVEN OFF IN THE STEAM ALONG WITH THE VOLATILE OILS. FOR THIS REASON, I SUGGEST PRESSURE COOKING FOR MOST VEGETABLES; ALSO, THE QUICK PRESSURE COOKING PRESERVES THE NATURAL COLOR OF THE VEGETABLE. OFTEN THE PRESSURE COOKER CAN BE USED WITHOUT THE CAP, AS THERE IS STILL MORE PRESSURE THAN THERE WOULD BE IN A KETTLE WITH THE CLOSEST-FITTING LID. SOME VEGETABLES TAKE ONLY A HALF MINUTE TO COOK IN THE PRES-SURE COOKER, SO IT IS A GOOD IDEA TO USE A TIMER IF YOU HAVE ONE. WHEN THE PRESSURE CAP IS USED, THE COOKER HAS TO BE COOLED IMMEDIATELY UNDER THE COLD WATER TAP TO PREVENT OVERCOOKING.

IN CHINA AND JAPAN THEY KNOW THE DELIGHT OF QUICKLY COOKED, CRISP VEGE-TABLES COOKED IN A WOK, A WONDERFUL COOKING GADGET. AS FAR AS I AM ABLE TO DISCOVER, VEGETABLES ARE COOKED BEST NOT IN EUROPE BUT IN AMERICA – ESPECIALLY IN CALIFORNIA. IN FRANCE, I EXPERIENCED THE HORROR OF GRAY, LIMP HARICOTS VERTS WITH NO SAUCE, NOT EVEN BUTTER; IT IS ALMOST SACRILEGE THUS TO RUIN THESE SMALL, TENDER BEANS.

Pan-Cooked Vegetables

For those who for one reason or another do not want to use a pressure cooker, here is an easy and uncomplicated way to prepare many vegetables. Use a large frying pan that can be tightly covered. Electric fry pans are excellent for this. Coat the vegetables with your favorite oil or melted butter, usually 2 to 4 tablespoons. Cook over low heat, stirring frequently and gently so that the vegetables do not stick. Most will provide their own juice. If some, like cabbage, are a little dry, add water sparingly, a tablespoon at a time. Keep the pan covered as much as possible.

The vegetables should be chopped or sliced thin. Any combination that appeals to you can be cooked together, but always start with an onion. Think of all the new and exotic flavor blends you can discover.

Further interest and flavor may be achieved by adding, singly or in combination, light seasonings such as ground turmeric or ground coriander, usually about 1/4 teaspoon, 1/2 teaspoon fresh grated ginger, or a few mustard seeds. If you use spices, add them to the oil or butter and cook slowly for a couple of minutes before adding the onion and sliced vegetables, so that the flavors will blend.

Vegetables cooked this way can be served with steamed rice, plain or with herbs or nuts added. A topping of plain yogurt is excellent.

Suggestion for Vegetable Variety

As a change to give variety to cooked vegetables, put a light layer of cottage cheese over them and heat covered, long enough for the cheese to get warm. For the vegetarian, this accompanied by rice topped with fresh yogurt provides adequate protein and good variation in flavors and textures.

**She should
eat yogurt.**

Collard Greens

You will often find these greens in your supermarket. If you don't, mustard greens will make a good substitute. Here is how they're served in New Orleans.

Wash carefully, taking off any tough stems, put into a kettle and press down a little:
1/2 teaspoon marjoram
2 bunches greens

Cube and brown lightly:
4 by 4–inch piece of fat
    salt pork

Put the browned pork cubes on top of the greens and pour the fat over them. This gives the real Southern flavor. Add enough water to make about 1 inch in the bottom of the pot, and cook covered until done. Serve with corn bread over which the "pot liquor" has been poured.

Serves 8

Beets Jamaica

Cut tops and tails from:
4 very large beets

Scrub beets and put them unpeeled through gricer, using medium cone. Cook in pressure cooker for 10 minutes at 15 pounds pressure with 1/4 cup water. If you do not have a gricer, put them in a pot with enough water to cover and boil until tender. Drain the water and slip off the skins. Slice very thin.

Blend together and stir until smooth:
3/4 teaspoon ground ginger or
    2 tablespoons freshly
    grated ginger
1/2 cup sugar
1 1/2 tablespoons cornstarch
1/2 cup cider vinegar

Cook 5 minutes, stirring constantly to prevent sticking. Add and simmer gently for 10 minutes to blend flavors, stirring occasionally:
the cooked beets
4 tablespoons butter

Serve piping hot, garnished with plenty of:
parsley, finely chopped

Serves 6

Holiday Cauliflower

Wash, trim and steam whole in covered kettle in 1 inch of water, until just done:
1 head cauliflower

Make bread crumbs by running through blender or crushing with rolling pin:
3 slices stale white bread

Melt:
1/4 pound butter

Add:
1/2 teaspoon herb salt
1/2 teaspoon curry powder,
  mixed with
  few drops garlic juice
bread crumbs

Stir mixture over low heat until a little dry and slightly browned. Drain head of cauliflower, set it in a shallow pan and cover the top generously with the bread crumbs. Make a ridge across the top with:
green peppers, chopped fine

Cross at right angles with a ridge of:
pimentos, chopped fine

Do all this while the cauliflower is still hot, and serve immediately – a festive way to serve vegetables.

Serves 6

Italian Artichokes

Cook in water for 45 minutes in saucepan or 10 minutes in pressure cooker at 15 pounds:
4 large artichokes
1 tablespoon olive oil
1 clove garlic
lemon juice

Remove, drain and separate leaves enough to sprinkle in the following mixture.

Heat until browned:
4 tablespoons butter
4 tablespoons olive oil
1 clove garlic, minced very fine
2 cups fine white bread crumbs

Toss with:
1/2 teaspoon herb salt
1/2 teaspoon dried marjoram

Divide mixture among the 4 artichokes, sprinkling it down into the leaves. Reheat in oven to serving temperature.

Serve with:
melted butter

Serves 4

Lima Bean Casserole

Put into pan with cover:
3 cups dry lima beans
water to cover 1 inch
    above beans

Bring to a boil, turn off heat and
allow beans to stand for 2 hours,
then drain and reserve excess liquid.

Simmer until done (*but not mushy*),
then add to beans:
4 tablespoons olive oil
2 cloves garlic, minced
2 carrots, sliced thin
2 large stalks celery, cut coarse
2 teaspoons fresh ginger root,
    minced

Mix together and add:
1 28–ounce can peeled tomatoes,
    slightly mashed
2 tablespoons brown sugar
1/4 cup drained bean water
1/4 cup Kikkoman soy sauce
4 sprigs marjoram
4 sprigs basil
2 sprigs thyme
4 sprigs cilantro
4 leaves costmary

Or, for the fresh herbs, substitute:
2 teaspoons savory herb blend
2 teaspoons salt

Bake in casserole for 2 hours at 325°
or until beans are thoroughly done.
If beans are not getting too mushy,
a longer cooking time will blend the
flavors better.

Serves 8 or more

Stuffed Baked Onions

Peel, slice the top off and scoop out the centers to make 1/2–inch thick shells:
4 very large Spanish onions

Mince:
center parts of onions

Mix with:
1 1/2 cups soft bread crumbs
4 tablespoons butter, melted
1/2 cup chopped walnuts
6 sprigs oregano
2 tablespoons parsley, minced
1/8 teaspoon white pepper
1/4 teaspoon salt

Be sure these ingredients are well mixed. Fill onion shells and arrange in baking pan. Blend and sprinkle over onions:
1/4 cup dry bread crumbs
2 tablespoons butter, melted
1/8 teaspoon basil

Bake in preheated oven at 350° for 40 minutes or until onions are tender but not soft.

Garnish with:
minced parsley
paprika

Serves 4

Eggplant Cairo

Simmer until onion is clear, not browned:
1/2 cup olive oil
3 cloves garlic, minced
1 large onion, chopped coarse
1 green pepper, chopped
1 teaspoon coriander, powdered
1 teaspoon turmeric
1/4 teaspoon cayenne
1 teaspoon fresh ginger root, minced
1/2 teaspoon powdered ginger
2 bay leaves *(discard after simmering)*

Add and stir in well while cooking so that it will absorb the oil:
1 medium eggplant, cut into 3/4–inch cubes

Now add:
1 28–ounce can tomatoes, cut up
1 vegetable bouillon cube
1 tablespoon brown sugar

Bake in casserole for 1 hour at 325°. Keep in warm oven for as much as 1 hour longer, if possible, to blend flavors. Rice and fresh yogurt, or cottage cheese, make a good accompaniment for this dish.

Serves 8

Russian Peasant Pie

Mix together:
2 cups all–purpose flour
2 teaspoons salt

Add and with fork press into
thin threads:
7 ounces butter

Mix butter into flour enough to
distribute it, then make a well
in the mixture and add:
2/3 cup cold buttermilk

Mix just until it all holds together,
then set aside.

Cook in covered kettle until just
done, not mushy:
1/2 pound butter
2 onions, sliced thin
1/2 small head of cabbage, cored
    and cut into 1–inch cubes
1 peeled turnip, sliced thin
2 peeled potatoes, sliced thin
1 large carrot, sliced very thin
2 cloves garlic, minced
2 teaspoons whole dill seeds
1 teaspoon savory herb blend

Combine over low heat:
2 tablespoons butter
3 tablespoons flour

Add and cook until thick; stir
constantly with wire whisk:
1 cup milk
1 vegetable bouillon cube

Add and mix gently into cooked
vegetables.

Chop and add:
1 cup any leftover meat
    (optional — the meat is not necessary
    as the vegetable mixture is rich and
    delicious by itself)

Set the mixture aside to cool.

Pie

The pie can be made in 1 large
baking dish or 2 smaller ones,
for this dish can be reheated in a
warm oven and comes out perfectly.
Roll out the dough very thin and
line the bottom and sides of the
baking dish.

Fill with cooled vegetables (*if they are
put in warm they tend to soak into the
bottom crust*). Moisten the edges of
the dough in the baking dish. Roll
out the top crust very thin and cover
the pie. Make 2 slits in the top to let
out the steam. Bake at 450° for 25
minutes or until top is nicely
browned. If directions have been
followed, the bottom crust should be
nicely browned also.

Serve garnished with yogurt. This
can be a complete meal in itself,
accompanied by a tossed green salad.

Serves 8

Steamed Vegetables

Put into frying pan that can be covered:

1/4 pound butter
1 tablespoon mustard seeds

Slowly fry the seeds so they won't burn, until they look a bit brown. Do not overcook them. Then add:

2 carrots, sliced
2 onions, cut coarse
2 stalks celery, cut coarse
1 zucchini, sliced
1 green pepper, chopped

When you can hear the vegetables sizzling, lift the lid slightly on one side and pour in:

1/4 cup hot water

Cover again instantly. The water will provide the steam to begin cooking the vegetables. Turn down the heat to low and continue to cook the vegetables until they are crisp, not mushy.

Add:
salt to taste

Serve with:
brown rice

Serves 6

See that the cooking time is short.

Chanterelle & Baby
Chard Strudel with Brie

Sauté until just tender:
**1 pound chanterelle
    mushrooms, thinly sliced
2 tablespoons butter**

When done, strain and save the mushroom juice.

In a separate pan sauté until very soft and the onions just start to caramelize:
**3 Spanish onions, thinly sliced
2 tablespoons garlic, minced
4 tablespoons butter**

Now add and continue to cook until just tender:
**1 large red bell pepper,
    chopped fine
4 cups baby Swiss chard,
    chopped fine
1/2 cup fresh basil leaves,
    minced**

When done, strain and save the vegetable juice.

Onion and mushroom mixture can be joined at this point and add:
**1/2 cup pine nuts, toasted
1/2 cup currants, which have
    been soaked in 1/4 cup white
    wine** (*wine from currants can
    be added to mushroom and
    vegetable juice*)

**1 teaspoon herb salt
1/2 teaspoon black pepper**

Chill mixture before making strudels.

Using 2 sheets of filo dough per strudel (*brushed lightly with butter between layers*) place:
**1 tablespoon Brie cheese
2 tablespoons of above filling**

Roll as for a burrito and slash several places on top to vent. Place in buttered non–stick baking pan and lightly brush the top of each strudel with butter. Bake at 400° about 15 minutes or until golden.

Sauce

Combine all vegetable juices and 1/2 cup of good white wine. Bring to a boil and simmer for a few minutes. Process 2 green onions and 6 to 8 large basil leaves in food processor with steel blade – add a bit of liquid toward the end. Add to saucepan and thicken slightly with butter and flour roux. Season with salt to taste and serve over hot strudels.

Serves 8

High Protein Stew

Prepare by slicing, then
braising slowly:
2 tablespoons butter
5 cloves garlic, minced
2 large onions, sliced coarse

When done add and continue to
cook slowly:
3 stalks celery, sliced
2 small carrots, sliced thin
2 zucchini, sliced
1/2 green sweet pepper, sliced
1/2 red sweet pepper, sliced
small potato, sliced (optional)

When done but not mushy add:
1 16–ounce can peeled tomatoes
1 16–ounce can red beans
1 16–ounce can corn niblets
seasoning with vegetable
**   herb blend**
herb salt to taste

Cook all ingredients slowly, then let
stand to blend flavors.

Serve in large soup bowls. Add
sprinkling of grated Cheddar cheese
to taste, if desired.

Serves 8

Butternut Squash

Pressure cook at 15 pounds
pressure for 5 minutes:
2 quarts butternut squash,
**   peeled, seeded, and then**
**   cut up**

In a saucepan heat together:
2 1/2 ounces brown sugar
1 teaspoon herb salt
2 1/2 ounces of ginger syrup
1/2 pound butter

Whip the squash and the
butter mixture well together
and serve warm.

Serves 12

Spanokopita

6 to 8 bunches spinach

Wash spinach until all of the grit has been removed. Using a large colander, tear spinach into it, and every bunch or so, sprinkle liberally with salt and rub it together with your hands. When finished with all of the spinach, let it sit for at least 1/2 hour. At that time, rinse spinach extremely well to remove as much of the salt as possible. Using a clean towel, twist handfuls of the spinach one at a time to remove as much liquid as possible. This is an important step, and must not be omitted or performed half–heartedly, or your end result will be a runny mess.

Sauté until done, then drain and set aside to cool:
1/4 cup olive oil
4 teaspoons minced garlic
2 large onions

When cool add and mix well together:
prepared spinach from
**   above, chopped**
2 tablespoons oregano
2 teaspoons black pepper
1 teaspoon dill weed
1 pound Feta cheese,
**   crumbled**
1/4 pound cream cheese,
**   crumbled**

Then add:
12 eggs, lightly beaten

To assemble, use:
1 pound filo dough
1/2 pound butter

Ideally filo dough should be removed from the freezer a day ahead of time and allowed to thaw in the refrigerator overnight. It should then be allowed to come to room temperature for at least 1 hour after it is taken from the refrigerator. The butter should be melted to brush the sheets of filo. The idea is to stack about 10 sheets of filo in the bottom of each pan, which must be buttered before starting. Also, each sheet of filo must be brushed with butter before placing on the next sheet.

Once the 10 sheets have been layered, put the filling in. Then layer another 3 to 6 sheets of filo over this, taking care to tuck the edges everywhere as much as possible so that the filling does not leak out. Bake at 350° approximately 1 hour.

Serves 8

Vegetable Cheese Soufflé

Braise until clear:
2 tablespoons olive oil
2 tablespoons butter
6 cloves garlic, minced
2 large onions, sliced very thin

When done add and cook until soft:
2 very large zucchini,
    sliced very thin
2 large carrots, sliced
    very thin
1 teaspoon vegetable herbs
2 teaspoons herb salt
1/8 teaspoon pepper

Beat together:
6 eggs
1/2 cup coffee cream

Add to cooked vegetables and stir
in until partly dissolved:
4 ounces aged Cheddar cheese,
    grated coarse

When cheese is partly melted
(*it should be cold from the refrigerator to
cool the vegetables so they will not curdle
the eggs mixture*), add the egg mixture
and stir in.

Turn into the casserole, 12 by 10
inches, and bake, after sprinkling
top with bread crumbs and paprika,
for about 30 minutes or until the
soufflé begins to raise up.

Serves 6

Apple & Date Stuffing

In a covered saucepan cook until
half done:
5 pippin apples, peeled,
    cored and quartered
1/2 cup water

When done set aside to cool, then
chop the apples fine, reserving
the juice.

In another covered saucepan
cook until tender:
1/4 pound dates,
    finely chopped
1/2 cup water

When done set aside to cool
and add:
1 tablespoon brandy

Combine apples, dates, and juice in
a mixing bowl and add:
4 cups bread crumbs,
    unseasoned
1/2 teaspoon savory
    herb blend
1/2 teaspoon herb salt
dash of pepper

Mix together and cool for stuffing.

To serve as a side dish, put in baking
pan and bake at 400° for 1/2 hour.

Peruska Periog

Mix together:
1 1/3 cups white flour
8 tablespoons butter
1 teaspoon salt

Make a well in the flour mixture and add:
1/3 cup buttermilk

Mix the dough until it will just hold together. Roll out thin and line an 8 by 8 by 1 1/2–inch baking dish. Reserve a little less than 1/2 for the top crust, which should be thick.

For the filling, mix together and cook until soft:
4 tablespoons butter
1 large onion, sliced thin
2 cups mushrooms, sliced coarse
3 cups cabbage, cut into 1/2–inch squares
1 1/2 teaspoons herb salt

Combine and stir gently into the cooked mixture:
8 hard–boiled eggs, peeled and cubed
1 1/2 cups Béchamel sauce
(*page 43*)

Spread mixture in lined baking dish and dot with butter. Roll out top crust and put over the mixture. Be sure to seal the edges to prevent boiling over. Make slits to release steam. Bake in a preheated 450° oven for about 25 minutes.

Serves 8

Herb Fried Potatoes

This is a version of the German Kartoffel Röesti.

Boil with skins on until just done, but not mushy:
6 potatoes

Peel potatoes and slice thin or put through gricer, coarse cone.

In a large frying pan melt:
1/4 pound butter

Spread potatoes in pan and put on top of them:
1 green pepper, chopped

Grind in mortar and sprinkle over potatoes:
1 sprig thyme
2 sprigs each of basil, marjoram and tarragon
2 leaves costmary
1 teaspoon onion salt
1/2 teaspoon garlic salt

Add:
plenty of chopped parsley

Fry potatoes until golden brown on the bottom. Before turning, dot with:
large pieces of butter

The herbs and peppers will steam, then brown lightly when the potatoes are turned. Plenty of butter is the secret. Cook uncovered, slowly so they won't burn. It may take 30 minutes.

Serve immediately to preserve the crispness of the potatoes.

Serves 6

Plenty of butter is the secret.

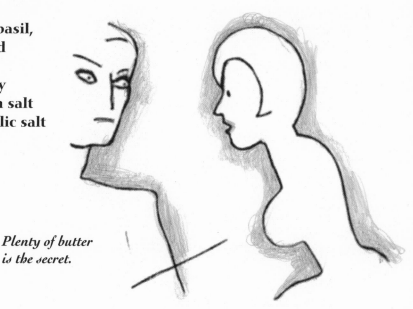

Potato Medley

Slice, or put through gricer, coarse cone; then toss together and put into a casserole that can be tightly covered:
2 large potatoes, peeled
2 large white turnips, peeled
2 large onions

Put on top of the vegetables:
thin slices of butter

Cover and bake at 400° until tender, about 30 minutes.

To prepare the sauce, combine over low heat:
1/4 pound butter
6 tablespoons flour

Grind together and add:
1 tablespoon herb salt
1 teaspoon savory
    herb blend

Add, cook and stir until thick:
3 cups milk

Pour the sauce over cooked vegetables and garnish with:
chopped parsley
paprika

Serves 4 to 6

Swiss-Style Yellow Wax Beans

Prepare by clipping ends and then cutting beans into 1 1/2-inch pieces:
2 pounds yellow wax beans

Cook very slowly until clear:
1 clove garlic, minced
2 tablespoons onion, chopped
2 tablespoons sweet butter

Mix together in pressure cooker and cook for 5 minutes without pressure cap or in covered pot until tender:
the prepared beans
onion and garlic mixture
1/2 cup water
3/4 teaspoon herb salt
1/2 teaspoon savory
    herb blend

When done the water should be all gone, and perhaps a little more will have to be added during the cooking to keep beans from sticking. Heat together gently to melt cheese:
3 ounces cream cheese
1/2 cup coffee cream

Add melted cheese to beans.

Serves 6

Tofu

It is strange that it took Americans so long to discover a most wonderful protein that has been used in China and Japan for centuries. It is called tofu and is known by other names like bean curd and bean cake. It is made from the milk of the soybean and comes packed and sealed in liquid.

By itself, tofu does not have much flavor and needs to be permeated by the flavors of other vegetables and seasonings; but it is a protein of such great food value and its texture is so marvelous that you will enjoy a feeling of well-being whenever you eat it.

Combinations using tofu are practically unlimited. When combining it with other vegetables, however, you must slice it or cut it into smaller squares and keep these from being broken up too much. In Japan it is often eaten as it is, with only a little soy sauce added.

I eat only soya products.

Tofu with Chinese Cabbage

Slice thin diagonally:
4 large leaves Chinese cabbage

Heat in pan that can be covered:
2 tablespoons peanut oil
1 tablespoon water

Add sliced cabbage leaves and cook until just done, not mushy.

Drain and cut into cubes:
1 pound tofu

Cook until just done, slightly crisp:
1 onion, sliced thin
1/4 cup peanut oil

Add and cook for 3 minutes:
1/2 pound mushrooms, sliced

Add and cook until thick:
1 cup water
3 tablespoons cornstarch
  (mixed in a little of the water)
1/4 cup soy sauce

Combine the cooked cabbage, tofu squares and the mushroom sauce, and let stand for a few minutes to blend flavors.

Serve with:
steamed rice

Serves 8

SEAFOOD

This is why my husband leaves home — such food!

$\mathcal{F}$RESH FISH SAUTÉED IN SWEET BUTTER, WITH A DASH OF HERB SALT AND A SQUEEZE OF LEMON OR LIME JUICE, MAKES A DISH FIT FOR ANY FOOD ENTHUSIAST. OF COURSE THIS IS NOT SUFFICIENT FOR ALL FISH, BUT IS DELICIOUSLY ADEQUATE FOR FILET OF SOLE OR THE LITTLE PERCH OR SUNFISH CAUGHT IN THE RIVERS OF THE MIDDLE WEST. OTHER, LARGER FISH NEED SOMETHING TO BRING OUT THEIR SPECIAL GOOD FLAVOR. WINE AND HERBS, USED IN VARIOUS COMBINATIONS, WILL DO THIS TO PERFECTION.

One of the best herbs to use with fish is tarragon. Another is fresh, chopped dill weed; its flavor, in combination with a dry white wine, brings something extraordinary to the dish. Sweet marjoram, basil, thyme, and especially borage are excellent. Summer savory in moderation, lovage and chives are also good. If the fish tends to be dry, sauces can be used to help it along. The flavor of the fish itself may be excellent, as is fresh salmon, but unless combined with something to offset the dryness, it will not be enjoyable.

Seafood Crêpes

Put into blender:

3 large eggs
2/3 cup carrot purée
    or broccoli purée
2/3 cup milk
2/3 cup water
1/4 teaspoon salt
3 teaspoons peanut oil
1/2 cup flour

Run until smooth, then add:

1/2 cup more flour

Continue to blend again until smooth. Let rest about 2 hours before using, to sufficiently cure flour.

Newburg Sauce
for Seafood Crêpes

Put into saucepan and heat to almost boiling:

2 quarts milk

Make the following roux:

1/2 cup flour
1/2 cup butter

Add roux to milk and cook until thick, then add and blend in:

1 cup chicken bouillon
1 1/2 teaspoons
    Worcestershire sauce
1 1/2 teaspoons dry mustard
1 1/2 teaspoons herb salt
1 teaspoon white pepper
1 1/2 teaspoons fish herb blend

Prepare crêpes and fill them with the above mixture; then add a small amount of poached fish (*any flaky-type fish will do*). Cook the filled crêpes slightly, just enough to reheat. Remove to serving plate which should have been heated previously. Spoon Hollandaise sauce (*page 37*) over the prepared crêpe and add to it:

1/2 cup tomato sauce

Serves 8

Halibut aux Fines Herbes

Place in a casserole:
8 slices halibut (*about 4 pounds*)

To make marinade, pound in mortar:
1 tablespoon herb salt
4 sprigs fresh tarragon
4 sprigs fresh lemon thyme
4 small leaves borage

Add herb mixture to:
1 cup white wine
3 tablespoons lemon juice

Mix well, then pour over the fish and marinate for at least 30 minutes. Drain off liquid and thicken slightly over low heat with:
1 tablespoon cornstarch, dissolved in a little water

Add:
3/4 cup fresh mushrooms, chopped fine
4 ounces mild Cheddar cheese, shredded

Spread mixture over fish in casserole and bake at 400° for about 25 minutes or until sauce begins to bubble evenly at the edges.

Garnish with:
thinly sliced toasted almonds
minced parsley

Serves 8

Halibut Escoffier

Break off bottom part and clean tops of:
18 asparagus spears

Stand asparagus in a tall vessel that can be tightly covered, add 1 cup water and steam until tender. Drain off water.

Combine in a saucepan:
4 tablespoons butter
8 tablespoons flour

Add, cook and stir until just thick:
1 cup whole milk
1 cup coffee cream
1 bay leaf (*discard when cooked*)

Mix together:
3 tablespoons white wine
1 1/2 teaspoons lemon juice
1/2 teaspoon herb salt

Add and mix into wine:
2 cups fresh mushrooms, sliced

Cover and heat just to boiling point, then simmer for 3 minutes. Add mushroom mixture to sauce and stir in well.

Halibut in Sour Cream with Dill

Place in a casserole:
6 servings of halibut filet

Sprinkle lightly with:
herb salt

Spoon the mushroom sauce over the halibut, then lay on each serving 3 asparagus spears. Bake at 400° until the sauce begins to bubble. Serve immediately, accompanied by a tossed green salad and fresh, cooked vegetables.

Serves 6

Pound in mortar:
2 tablespoons fresh dill, chopped fine
1 leaf costmary, minced
1 leaf French sorrel
1 small sprig lemon thyme, chopped
1 teaspoon herb salt

Mix ground herbs into:
1 cup sour cream

Place in buttered casserole:
4 halibut filets

Add sour cream sauce and bake at 400° until just bubbling. Serve immediately, topping each portion with a sprig of dill. Provide lemon wedges for extra tartness if desired.

Serves 4

Halibut Toledo

Sauté until tender:
1/2 cup olive oil
8 teaspoons minced garlic
2 red onions, thinly sliced

When done add and simmer to blend flavors:
4 cans tomatoes, seeded
    and coarsely chopped
4 vegetable bouillon cubes
1 teaspoon lemon thyme,
    ground, in
    1 teaspoon salt
4 teaspoons fresh dill,
    minced
3 cups ripe olives,
    cut in half

Serve sauce under charbroiled fresh halibut.

Serves 8

Poached Salmon with Caper Sauce

Lay in baking dish:
6 fresh salmon slices,
    1 inch thick

Sprinkle with:
herb salt

Pour around salmon (*but do not quite cover it*):
white wine

Cover baking dish with wax paper. Do not use foil. Poach at 400° for about 8 minutes or until wine is bubbling well. Remove from oven. Discard juice.

To make sauce, mix well together:
1 1/2 cups Béchamel sauce
    (*page 43*)
1/2 cup capers
1/2 cup coffee cream
1/2 teaspoon herb salt
2 tablespoons dry Sauterne

Put salmon in casserole and spoon caper sauce over it. Bake at 400° until sauce bubbles.

Serves 6

Poached Salmon with
Red Wine & Mushrooms

Lay in baking dish:
**8 fresh salmon slices,
    about 1 inch thick**

Dot with:
butter

Squeeze over salmon:
lemon juice

Broil salmon until it begins
to brown a little. Remove and
keep warm.

Braise in a little butter:
2 green onions, chopped fine
2 shallots, chopped fine
2 stalks celery, chopped fine
**2 ounces fresh mushrooms,
    sliced thin**

Pound in mortar, then add to
above and mix well:
2 sprigs marjoram
2 sprigs lemon thyme
**2 leaves costmary or
    1/2 leaf mint**
1/2 teaspoon herb salt

Cover salmon with this mixture,
then pour around it but do not
quite cover with:
red wine

Cover dish with wax paper, fitting
paper tightly. Do not use foil.
Bake about 10 minutes at 400°,
or until done. Remove paper and
drain juice.

To juice, add:
1/2 pound butter
Reheat juice to almost boiling.

Put in blender:
2 egg yolks (*at room temperature*)

Start blender and add quickly
salmon juice and butter while
bubbling hot and:
dash of herb salt

Blend about 15 seconds – no longer.
Serve over warm poached salmon.

Garnish with:
parsley

Serves 8

Court Bouillon

Sauté for 3 minutes:
1/3 cup carrots, diced small
1/3 cup celery, diced small
1/3 cup onion, diced small
2 large sprigs parsley
2 tablespoons butter

Add and bring to the boiling point:
6 peppercorns
2 cloves
1/2 bay leaf
1 tablespoon salt
2 tablespoons vinegar or
    8 ounces dry white wine
2 quarts water

(When poaching fish,
this recipe is excellent.)

Poached Chilled Salmon

Lay in baking dish:
salmon filets, cut into
    serving pieces

Sprinkle with herb salt and pour
around them but do not quite cover:
1/4 cup white wine
3/4 cup water

Cover baking dish with waxed paper.
Poach at 350° for 20 minutes. Remove
from oven. Drain juice and reserve.
Place salmon in refrigerator and chill
for 24 hours.

Sauce

Place in blender and mix:
2/3 cup fish juice from above
1/2 teaspoon dry mustard
2 teaspoons fish herb blend
1 teaspoon dill
2 teaspoons herb salt
2 tablespoons vinegar
dash white pepper

Pour into bowl, add and stir well:
2 pounds sour cream
1 cucumber *(that has been sliced very*
    thin and allowed to stand for 15
    minutes with salt and then washed,
    to take out the excess water)
1 cup watercress, minced

Chill sauce well before using.
Garnish with watercress and a few
slices of fresh cucumber.

Broiled Salmon
with Sauce Alsace

Slice thin:
2/3 cup fresh mushrooms

Butter lightly a very heavy iron
skillet (*a thin one will cause the fish
to dry out during broiling*).

Lay close together in pan:
**6 slices salmon, 1 to 1 1/4 inches
thick, lightly salted**

Broil salmon on first side for
7 minutes.

While salmon is broiling, put in
blender and whirl for 2 minutes:
1/2 tablespoon celery seeds
1/2 tablespoon poppy seeds
1/2 tablespoon sesame seeds
3/4 teaspoon onion salt
1/8 teaspoon peppercorns
3 gratings fresh nutmeg

Melt and add to mixture in blender
and run for 1/2 minute:
1/2 pound butter, melted

Turn the slices of salmon gently so
as not to break them. They have two
long ends extending from the belly
of the fish. Put into the belly cavity
of each salmon slice 1/6 of the sliced
mushrooms, and wrap the long ends
around them, making a small oasis
of mushrooms in the steak.

Squeeze over the salmon:
a few drops lemon juice

Salt lightly with:
herb salt

Spoon sauce over salmon steaks
and broil second side for 3 minutes.
Serve immediately.

Serves 6

Filet of Sole Béarnaise

Season filets of sole to taste with
herb salt and brown lightly on
both sides in butter. Do not overcook
the sole. Spoon Béarnaise sauce
(*page 38*) over the sole and serve
immediately.

Filet of Sole au Gratin

Place filets of sole in casserole (*halibut is also good*). Spoon cheese sauce (*page 172*) over the sole and bake for 10 to 15 minutes at 400° until the sauce bubbles well at the edges.

Serve immediately.

Fiskepudding (Fish Mousse)

This dish makes a great first course for a large dinner. If possible, bake the mousse in a fish mold, which can be obtained in gourmet and gift shops.

Put into blender:

1 pound filet of sole (*or any tender white fish*)
2 cups coffee cream
1/4 cup dry vermouth
1/4 teaspoon nutmeg
1 tablespoon herb salt
2 teaspoons lemon or lime juice
4 eggs

Run until well mixed, at least 2 minutes, then add and continue mixing:

3 tablespoons potato starch
(*cornstarch will not do*)

Bake at 325° in greased pan or mold set in a shallow pan with 1 inch of boiling water in it, like a double boiler. Bake until pudding is firm in the middle, about 1 hour.

To prepare sauce for pudding, heat together gently:

2 cups sour cream
1/2 teaspoon herb salt
1 teaspoon fresh dill weed, chopped fine

After the pudding is baked, run a knife blade around the inside edge of the mold, and place over the top of the mold a large platter which has been thoroughly warmed. Then turn over the mold and platter, and the pudding will drop into it. Serve the sauce in a bowl.

Serves 5 to 6

Variation: Salmon Fiskepudding

My sister Dorothy had been doing some food photography with fresh salmon and had brought us some that was left over, which we put in the freezer. Here was a chance to experiment, so we defrosted the salmon and used it in place of the white fish. The resulting mousse was a great success, delicious and a wonderful pink.

Filet of Sole Mimosa

I was in Paris in the spring, and I know why they call this "Sole Momosa" for it does look like the flowering Mimosa tree when served properly.

Sauté:
2 shallots, chopped fine
2 tablespoons butter

Add and simmer for 5 minutes:
4 tablespoons cooked veal,
minced
4 mushrooms, chopped fine
4 sprigs parsley
4 sprigs marjoram
2 sprigs thyme
1 leaf costmary *(optional)*

Add and simmer again for 5 minutes:
2 cups chicken stock
1/4 cup Chablis or other
white wine
1/2 teaspoon herb salt
1/2 teaspoon lemon juice

Thicken with:
4 tablespoons flour mixed
in a little water

Fry in butter until just done
(do not overcook):
3 pounds filet of sole,
very fresh

Sprinkle lightly with:
herb salt

Lay cooked sole on hot platter and spoon sauce over it.

Garnish

Hardboil:
3 eggs

Separate and put through a sieve the whites and yolks of the eggs and *(here is the Mimosa touch)* sprinkle in alternate rows of white and yellow over the fish.

Serves 6

Sole Stuffed with Baby Shrimp

Have ready:
4 pounds filet of Petrale sole

Sauté:
3 shallots, chopped fine
3 tablespoons chicken fat

Add and simmer gently for
5 minutes:
1 tablespoon minced ham
4 mushrooms, chopped fine
4 sprigs parsley, chopped fine
1/4 teaspoon fish herb blend

Mix together and add:
1/2 cup Chablis
1/2 teaspoon herb salt
2 envelopes George Washington
   golden seasoning
   (available in most markets)
2 cups Béchamel sauce *(page 43)*

Add and simmer again for 5 minutes:
4 cups cooked cocktail shrimp

Spread this mixture on the sole
filets, roll them up and place them
in a casserole. Spoon over rolls:
2 cups cheese sauce *(page 172)*

Bake at 400° until sauce begins
to bubble.

Serves 8

Filet of Sole Florentine

Chop very fine:
1 10–ounce package frozen
   or 2 bunches raw spinach

Cook in very little water for
1 minute. Drain and add:
1 teaspoon herb salt

Spread a light bed of the cooked
spinach in a casserole and place on
top of it:
8 servings filet of sole

Mix together and spread over
the sole:
1 1/2 cups Béchamel sauce
   (page 43)
1 1/2 cups coffee cream
1 1/2 cups very sharp
   Cheddar cheese, grated
1/2 teaspoon Worcestershire
   sauce
dash herb salt
dash cayenne pepper
2 teaspoons sherry

Bake at 400° until the sauce begins to
bubble around the edges. Remove,
garnish and serve immediately.

Serves 8

Filet of Sole with
Bercy Capers Sauce

Bring the following to a boil:
1 1/3 cups fish stock
1 pound butter, melted
1/4 teaspoon fish herb blend

Heat a blender bowl with hot water
to warm, and discard the water.
Put egg yolks in the blender, add
the boiling liquid to the yolks with
blender running. Whirl for a few
seconds only:
6 egg yolks

Remove blender and fold
in until smooth:
1 cup Béchamel sauce
(page 43)
6 tablespoons capers,
well drained

Lightly poach the filet
of sole and spoon
the sauce over it, or
serve it on the side.

Serves 6

*Yes, my wife
is out of town.*

Sole Veronique

Combine in a saucepan:
4 tablespoons butter
4 tablespoons flour

Add, cook and stir until thick
and smooth:
1 pint coffee cream
1/2 bay leaf (discard when cooked)
1/2 teaspoon herb salt

Add and mix in well:
1 beaten egg yolk
dash white pepper
2 teaspoons sherry
2 ounces small white
**   seedless grapes**

Wash thoroughly:
2 pounds filet of sole

Lay filets in casserole and
sprinkle lightly with:
herb salt

Spoon sauce over sole and bake at
400° until sauce begins to bubble.
(*If you happen to have Béchamel sauce
(page 43) on hand, you can use it in place
of the above sauce, adding the wine
and grapes.*)

Garnish with:
parsley, chopped fine
lemon, sliced thin
paprika

Serves 6

Sole Farnham

Scald, preparing to peel, and seed:
1 cup ripe tomatoes, cut into
**   1/2-inch pieces**

Bring to boil and reduce to
half volume:
1 quart whipping cream

Bring to boil and reduce to half:
1 cup white wine

Add to whipping cream which
is reduced.

Now add and stir in:
3 tablespoons minced
**   sorrel leaves**
1 teaspoon herb salt
cut up tomatoes

Broil for each serving:
6 ounces English sole
herb salt sprinkled on top

Put above sauce in casserole, lay
broiled sole on sauce and add a
small amount on top, then sprinkle
on sauce:
minced sorrel
few drops lemon or lime juice

Serves 6

Red Snapper with Herbs

Braise lightly to set juices:
2 pounds filet of red snapper
4 tablespoons butter

Cook until tender:
1 small green onion,
   chopped fine
1 tablespoon butter

Grind in mortar, then add to cooked onion:
1 teaspoon herb salt
2 small leaves (*or 1 large leaf*)
   borage
2 sprigs marjoram
2 sprigs lemon thyme
3 leaves costmary
1 leaf lemon balm
2 sprigs tarragon
2 sprigs dill

Mix together and add to herbs, then cook until thick:
1 tablespoon lemon juice
2 tablespoons cornstarch
1 cup white wine
1 egg yolk
1 tablespoon sunflower
   seeds (*optional*)

Place braised fish in buttered casserole and pour sauce over it. Bake at 400° only until sauce bubbles. Do not overcook as fish flakes easily.

Garnish with:
minced parsley
paprika

Serves 4

Red Snapper
with Borage Sauce

Place in baking pan:
6 servings (*about 3 pounds*)
   red snapper filets

Sprinkle with:
1 large leaf borage, minced
1/2 teaspoon fish herb blend

Cover with wax paper and bake for
20 minutes at 350°. Drain off juice
and add, if necessary, enough water
to make 2/3 cup liquid.

Add to fish liquid and bring
to boil:
1/2 pound butter

Put liquid in warmed blender
with:
2 egg yolks

Whirl for 10 seconds, no more.
Put baked fish in attractive casserole
and pour sauce over it. Reheat to
serving temperature. Raw pine nuts
(*pignolias*) may be added for texture.

Serves 6

Red Snapper Milano

Sauté in pan:
4 tablespoons butter
1 cup green onions, minced
1 cup celery hearts, minced
1 tablespoon tarragon, minced
1 tablespoon rosemary, minced
1 tablespoon basil, minced

Bring to boil to reduce by 1/3:
3 cups red wine
3 cups fish juice
1/2 cup red wine vinegar
2 tablespoons sugar
dash white pepper
dash clove
1/2 teaspoon herb salt

Combine all the above and strain.
Then thicken with starch to desired
consistency. Serve over broiled
fresh red snapper with marinated
artichokes and marinated sliced
mushrooms, and a side order
of pasta.

Serves 8

Red Snapper Creole

Sauté until done:
1/2 cup olive oil
4 cups onions, chopped
4 cups celery, chopped
2 cloves garlic, minced

Now add:
2 cups parsley, chopped
1/2 teaspoon dry thyme,
pulverized
6 ounces tomato paste
2 1/2 teaspoons salt

Add and simmer for 20 minutes:
46 ounces tomato juice
1/2 teaspoon black pepper
1/4 teaspoon ground nutmeg
1/2 teaspoon cayenne pepper

Drain liquid and save vegetables in separate container.

Thicken juice with 1/4 cup starch and cook until smooth. When this sauce is cooked properly, it will cling to the fish when poured over it.

Put spoons of cooked vegetables in casserole and then lay fish on them, spooning sauce over fish before baking until sauce bubbles around the edges. Do not overcook.

Serves 8 to 10

Clams Florentine

Drain and reserve juice from:
3 7 1/2–ounce cans
minced clams

Cook until clear:
3 green onions, minced fine
1/4 pound butter

Mix together:
3/4 cup white wine
clam juice

Cook until reduced by half, then add to cooked onions. Cook 1 minute in covered saucepan in very little water (*almost none*):
3 bunches spinach (*tops only*)

While spinach is cooking, mix:
4 tablespoons cornstarch,
mixed in a little water
1/2 cup whipping cream
1/2 teaspoon salt
1/4 teaspoon nutmeg

Combine with clam–broth mixture and cook until thickened, then combine with clams. Make a bed of the cooked spinach in a casserole and sprinkle it with:
herb salt

Spoon on the clam mix and top with:
1/2 cup grated Parmesan cheese
1/2 cup grated, aged Swiss
cheese

Bake at 400° for 15 minutes or until sauce begins to bubble. Garnish with thin twisted slices of lemon.

Serves 6

Crab Voisin

This is a true story, and of all the incidents related in this book, it is surely the most unusual. Inda and Jack Lynes, friends of my sister Dorothy, were up from Los Angeles one evening. Jack asked me if I would like to submit a recipe in a contest which was being arranged.

"If I should win, what would the prize be?" I asked.

"It's pretty fancy," he said, "an all-expense-paid gourmet tour for you and your wife for two weeks, to London and Paris."

"I don't think I would be able to get away for that long right now. And if I won and could go, I'd probably eat myself to death — so I guess I must pass up the opportunity."

"Well, then, would you like to be one of the judges? Before you accept, however, perhaps you should know more about the whole thing. Depending on how you feel, there may be a slight drawback…"

The contest was being sponsored by the Avocado Advisory Board, he told me, and invitations to submit recipes were sent by Earl MacAusland, editor of Gourmet Magazine, to well-known chefs all over the United States. Over three hundred recipes had been submitted. There were to be three judges: an executive chef, an amateur chef, and someone who writes about food.

"You've just published a cookbook, so you qualify," Jack said, and continued: "The first two judges have been selected. The executive chef will be Hans Prager of Lawrey's Foods. The amateur chef is Sebastian Cabot of TV and film fame.

For the third judge Lucius Beebe had been chosen, but he died. Then," Jack went on slowly, "we asked Art Ryon who wrote the dining out column for the Los Angeles Times. He died."

"Wow!" I said, "I see what you mean — but I'm not superstitious. I'll be the third man."

The contest was to be judged in the executive suite of TWA in Los Angeles. The night before I was to go there, I was sitting in my room reading the newspaper. Suddenly, I began to feel very ill, so much so I had to lie down on the bed. Of course, I thought about the third-man superstition, but I told myself it was absolutely ridiculous. Eventually the illness passed and I was all right. The next morning, just so I wouldn't get bored, I asked a friend to go to Los Angeles with me. And I drove very, very carefully…

There were quite a few people gathered about and cameras clicking as we did the judging, and we finally agreed on one dish made with crab and avocado. The number on the dish identified it as the entry of Hippolyte Haultcouer, executive chef of the Voisin Restaurant in New York. He was called and told that he was the winner of the contest.

It was some time before I saw Jack and Inda again. My first question, of course, was "How did Hippolyte and his wife enjoy their trip?" "They didn't go."

"Didn't go! Why not?"

"Because," Jack said, "he died."

Here is the winning recipe. I have changed it a little to suit our restaurant.

Prepare the following rich cream sauce.

Combine in a saucepan:
3 tablespoons butter
3 tablespoons flour

Add and cook until thick:
1 1/4 cups coffee cream
1 bay leaf *(discard when cooked)*
1/2 teaspoon herb salt

When thick, add and mix in well:
1 egg yolk
dash white pepper

To half of the cream sauce add and mix together well:
1 cup cooked crab meat, flaked
1 cup cooked rice
2 tablespoons pignolia nuts, raw

Halve and peel:
4 avocados

Put the avocado halves in a casserole and fill each half with the crab mixture, heaping it up.

Put the other half of the cream sauce in a double boiler.

Add and mix in well:
1/3 cup aged sharp Cheddar cheese, shredded
1 1/2 tablespoons coffee cream
1 1/2 tablespoons sherry

Cook until cheese is melted, then spoon sauce over crab mixture. Bake at 400° only until sauce starts to bubble. Do not overcook, as avocados will then develop an acid taste. They should only be heated through. This is a very rich dish so allow only half an avocado per person.

Serves 8

I'll be the third man.

Crab Acapulco

Prepare fettuccini noodle dough with part white flour and part cornmeal. Boil until just tender.

Prepare mixture as follows:
1/4 cup sliced black olives
1 1/2 cups crabmeat
1/4 cup pimentos,
    cubed small
1 green bell pepper, cut
    into strips and braised
1/4 cup green olives,
    diced
1 cup rice, cooked
1 cup Béchamel sauce *(page 43)*
1/2 cup seeded, chopped
    tomatoes

Mix all of the ingredients together very well and serve on a bed of the above cooked noodles.

Serves 6

Crab Fujiyama

Prepare by cooking and shelling:
1 pound crab meat, shredded

Add and mix well:
4 cups Béchamel sauce
    (page 43)

Spoon this mixture onto small squares of buttered toast in casserole, or into scallop shells for individual servings. Bake at 400° until crab bubbles at edges. Serve immediately.

Serves 6

Mushrooms Stuffed with Crab

Mix together thoroughly:
1 pound crab meat, shredded
1/2 cup Monterey jack cheese,
   shredded
1 egg white, beaten lightly
1 tablespoon white wine
1/2 teaspoon herb salt
dash cayenne pepper

Combine and add, mixing in
thoroughly:
1 cup soft white bread crumbs
1/2 cup Béchamel sauce (*page 43*)

Clean and remove stems from:
18 very large mushrooms

Place mushrooms right side up
in well–buttered skillet, cover tightly
and cook over low heat until they
are just slightly soft to the touch.
Turn the mushrooms over and
salt them lightly with:
herb salt

Using a small scoop to shape it,
put a scoop of the stuffing on each
mushroom and top with a small
amount of:
Monterey jack cheese

Bake at 400° until the mushrooms
begin to simmer.

Have ready:
rounds of white toast,
   well buttered

Place mushrooms on toast.
Serve immediately, 3 to a serving.

Serves 6

(*If your guests feel at home enough to call
for seconds, perhaps you had better have
extras ready!*)

*They asked
for seconds.*

Scampi Alassio

This dish takes some time to prepare, but it is so good I think you will find it worth the extra effort. It was first served to me in a waterfront restaurant in Alassio, Italy. The restaurant itself is old and the building dates from the 12th century. Because it is on the waterfront all of the ironwork — hinges, rods, fasteners and such — are weathered and rust pitted and have the wonderful patina of great age. At one end of the room are tables made of the coarsest heavy wood. No dividing wall separates the dining area from the kitchen at the other end of the room. You can watch the chef prepare the food. In the middle of his work area is a great chopping block such as one sees in butcher shops, and at one side in a brick wall is a fireplace where much of the food is cooked.

Cook for 3 minutes only in boiling water:
32 large shrimp
2 bay leaves

Overcooking will toughen the shrimp. Discard bay leaves; shell and devein the shrimp.

Mix together and cook until done but not mushy:
1/4 cup olive oil
1 stalk celery, chopped very fine
1 green pepper, chopped
   very fine
1 small carrot, chopped very fine
3 green onions, chopped
   very fine
1/4 teaspoon fish herb blend
1/4 teaspoon herb salt

Combine in another pan:
3 tablespoons butter
3 tablespoons flour

Add, then cook and stir until thick:
1/2 cup milk
1/4 cup coffee cream
a small piece of bay leaf
   (discard when cooked)

Add to cooked sauce:
3/4 cup cooked and
   flaked crabmeat

Combine vegetables and sauce and spread on a bed of:
cooked rice

Shrimp Creole

Keep warm.

Put into a small frying pan and cook for 1/2 minute:
2 cloves garlic, minced fine
2 tablespoons olive oil

Remove and discard the garlic. Put the boiled shrimp in the oil and cook until heated through, then add:
1/4 cup brandy

Flame the shrimp by heating the brandy and then tipping the pan until the alcohol catches fire. When the flames die down, lay the shrimp on top of the vegetable and crab mixture and pour the juice from the pan over the entire dish.

Serves 4

Cook in pressure cooker without cap, or until just done but not mushy:
1 green pepper, cut coarse
1 clove garlic, minced
1 large onion, about 1 cup, cut very coarse
1 cup celery, cut coarse
2 bay leaves (*discard when cooked*)
1/2 cup chopped parsley
1/4 teaspoon thyme
dash cayenne pepper

When done, add:
1/3 cup tomato paste
1 teaspoon salt

Reheat and adjust seasoning with salt.

Fry until clear:
2 cloves garlic, minced
4 tablespoons olive oil

Add and cook only enough to thoroughly heat through:
1 pound cooked, peeled and deveined shrimp, seasoned with 1/2 teaspoon herb salt
2 turns from pepper mill

Mix shrimp with vegetable sauce. Serve hot with rice.

Serves 8

Shrimp Peking

Boil 5 pounds frozen shrimp
(*broken pieces*) for 2 minutes, drain
and mix well with:
3 tablespoons soy sauce
1 1/2 teaspoons fresh ginger,
   minced fine
3 cloves garlic, minced fine

Place wok on high heat for about
1 minute. Put in 1 tablespoon
peanut oil. When hot add
1/3 shrimp mixture and stir fry for
2 to 3 minutes. Repeat twice more
using remaining thirds each time.

Prepare:
12 stalks celery, 1/4-inch slices
3 onions sliced thin, then across
8 ounces water chestnuts, sliced
4 cups fresh bean sprouts

Sauce (*leave cold until ready to serve*):
6 tablespoons starch
3/8 teaspoon white pepper
6 tablespoons soy sauce
1 1/2 cups chicken broth
6 tablespoons Saki

To serve: Stir fry for 2 minutes the
celery and onion and steam. Add 1
serving of shrimp. Stir fry until hot,
then add 1 1/2 ounces of the sauce
and cook until thick. Fold in the
water chestnuts and bean sprouts.
Serve with rice and soy sauce.

Serves 12

Shrimp Blintzes

Put in saucepan and add boiling
water to cover, and boil 3 minutes:
1 pound frozen shrimp
2 bay leaves
1 teaspoon salt

Drain, peel and devein shrimp
and chop them very fine.
Discard bay leaves.

Put in saucepan:
1 tablespoon lemon juice
2 tablespoons melted butter

Mince and add to butter:
2 stalks celery
3 green onions and tops
large sprig tarragon
3 large leaves basil
3 sprigs thyme
3 sprigs savory (*or a dash*)
1 1/4 teaspoons herb salt

Braise until onions are done and
celery is still slightly crisp, then mix
with the shrimp and add:
2 cups Béchamel sauce (*page 43*)

Prepare crêpes (*page 133*). Place a
heaping tablespoon of shrimp on
brown side of each crêpe (*only one side
fried first*) and roll, tucking in ends.
Fry in butter until golden brown on
each side. Serve with sour cream.

Serves 4 to 6

Curried Shrimp,
Indian Style

Prepare a massala (*spice mixture*) by grinding in blender until fine (*or pound in mortar*):

1 tablespoon mustard seed
4 whole cloves
3/4 teaspoon poppy seeds
3/4 teaspoon peppercorns
**1 1/2 teaspoons ground
  cardamom** (*or 5 whole seeds*)
3/4 teaspoon turmeric powder

Cook until clear (*about 2 minutes*):

2 tablespoons butter
1/2 onion, minced fine
2 cloves garlic, minced

Add spice mixture and continue to cook very slowly until thick. Add and simmer for at least 15 minutes more:

1/2 cup coconut milk

Add and continue to cook until thoroughly heated, stirring frequently:

**2 1/2 pounds cooked shrimp,
  peeled and deveined**

Cook in pressure cooker for about 1 minute without the pressure cap (*or in covered saucepan until tender but still crisp*):

1/4 cup water
3 stalks celery, sliced coarse
2 onions, cut coarse
1 green pepper, cut coarse
(*vegetables should be in large pieces for texture*)

Mix the cooked, drained vegetables into the shrimp and massala mixture, and reheat over water. Do not allow to get too hot, as the chrimp will take on an unpleasant flavor if heated too much and too long.

Add and continue to keep hot for about 15 minutes to blend flavors:

1/2 cup buttermilk
1/2 cup sour cream
1/2 teaspoon salt

Adjust seasoning with salt, and serve with saffron rice, chutney and other condiments.

Serves 8

Sea Bass Portugal

Cook until clear, in 1 cup olive oil:
6 large onions
10 cloves garlic

Mince and add:
8 sprigs oregano
8 sprigs lemon thyme
8 sprigs basil
4 sprigs rosemary

Then add and cook for 2 minutes:
1 cup vinegar
2 cups white wine
2 quarts chicken broth

Drain liquid, bring to a boil and add:
1 tablespoon dry mustard
1/2 teaspoon white pepper
1 tablespoon salt *(salt to taste*
   with chicken broth)
1/2 cup sugar
1/2 cup lemon juice
2 teaspoons turmeric
3/4 cup Dijon mustard

Thicken with cornstarch and water.

Combine all ingredients and add:
1/4 cup chopped parsley
1/4 cup chopped celery tops

To serve, place small amount of sauce on plate under broiled or grilled sea bass or halibut. Garnish with:
marinated red onions
parsley

Marinated Red Onions

Bring to a boil:
2 cups white wine
1 cup water
1/2 cup apple cider vinegar
1/2 cup sugar
1 teaspoon salt
1 teaspoon dry mustard
dash white pepper
1/4 cup lemon juice

Then add:
sliced red onions

Cook until just done. Remove onions, drain and place in stainless steel pan. Refrigerate. *(Saved marinade can be used again.)*

Serves 16

Sea Bass Tampico Mayonnaise

Put in blender and blend for
2 or 3 minutes:
2 whole eggs
1 cup tarragon leaves
2 teaspoons dry mustard
2 teaspoons herb salt
2 teaspoons sugar
2 teaspoons cayenne pepper
2 tablespoons minced garlic
1/2 cup olive oil

Now gradually add and continue
to blend in this order:
1 cup olive oil
then:
3/4 cup lime juice
then:
1 cup olive oil

Broil fish until almost done and
spread on some of the mayonnaise.
Continue broiling until slightly
browned.

Serves 6

Lobster with Lemon Thyme Butter

*If you have an herb garden — and even
a tiny one is a treasure beyond calculation —
it should contain lemon thyme, which goes
on year after year, so that it is always
available.*

Split:
2 lobsters, cooked and cleaned

Lay lobster in broiling pan and
coat generously with the following
butter sauce.

Put in blender:
1/2 pound melted butter
1/2 teaspoon herb salt
6 sprigs lemon thyme

Run until blended, about 1 minute.

Broil coated lobster until it begins
to brown slightly. Do not overcook
as the lobster tends to dry out
and toughen.

Serve with:
drawn butter
lemon wedges

Serves 4

Lobster Thermador

Prepare by cooking for about 30 minutes, and then removing meat from shell:

**3 pounds cooked,
    fresh lobster, shelled**

Mix lobster with:
2 quarts Béchamel sauce
    (page 43)
4 tablespoons sherry

Put in baking dish and if desired, sprinkle with:
grated Cheddar cheese

Bake about 10 minutes to bubbling point and then put under broiler last few minutes to slightly brown top if cheese has been added.

Serves 8

Scallops Espagnole

Put into a pot that can be covered:
1/4 cup olive oil
2 cloves garlic, minced

Cook until clear then add, in the order named:
4 stalks celery, cut coarse
2 onions, cut coarse
2 green peppers, cut coarse
1/4 cup parsley, chopped fine
1/2 teaspoon basil
1/2 teaspoon marjoram
1/4 teaspoon thyme
1/4 teaspoon black pepper
2 sprigs cilantro, minced

Cook vegetables until just done but not mushy; then add and bring to boil:
**1 28–ounce can tomatoes,
    mashed**
3 pimentos, chopped
1 teaspoon lemon or lime juice

Prepare:
1 cup rice

Deep fry:
1 pound breaded scallops

Make a bed of rice in a casserole, put the scallops on it and pour the vegetable sauce over them, heaping it in the center so that the scallops show around the edges. Serve hot.

Serves 4

Scallops & Crab
with Sweet Herbs

Mix together in a pan with a cover:
1 pound scallops
1 tablespoon white wine
dash white pepper
1/2 bay leaf (*discard when cooked*)

Grind together and add to scallops:
1/4 teaspoon herb salt
1 sprig thyme
1 sprig marjoram
1 shallot, minced

Simmer scallops very slowly for
5 minutes.

Cook for 2 minutes, gently:
2 cups sliced fresh mushrooms
1 tablespoon white wine

Combine in a saucepan:
3 tablespoons butter
3 tablespoons flour

Add, cook and stir until thick:
1 cup milk
1 cup coffee cream

Add scallops and mushrooms to
sauce, then mix in:
1/2 pound cooked,
   shredded crab

Put mixture into casserole and
bake at 400° until sauce begins to
bubble, then top with:
mild, grated cheese

Place under broiler and brown
lightly.

Serves 6

Scallops St. Jacques Provençal

Boil for 10 minutes, peel and set aside:
2 eggs

Mix together:
1/4 cup white wine
1/4 cup water
1 small clove garlic,
   minced very fine
1 shallot, chopped fine
1/4 teaspoon salt
1/8 teaspoon fresh–ground
   black pepper

Add to mixture:
1 pound scallops

Simmer scallops gently for about 5 minutes. Drain off juice and reserve. If there is more than 1 cup, boil to reduce to that amount. If there is less, add water to make 1 cup.

Add to juice:
1/4 cup whipping cream
1/4 teaspoon herb salt

Combine:
2 tablespoons butter
2 tablespoons flour

Add to juice mixture, cook and stir until thick, then add:
1 teaspoon lemon juice

Cut boiled eggs into quarters lengthwise, then once across the center. Add scallops to sauce, then gently mix in the eggs.

Cook in tightly covered pan until tender:
1 small carrot, shredded
1 small green pepper,
   cut in thin strips
2 tablespoons butter

Put scallop mixture in casserole and garnish with carrot and green pepper mixture. Add in a decorative ring:
cherry tomatoes

Bake at 400° until sauce begins to bubble. Serve immediately.

Serves 4

Scallops Provençal

Drain scallops and save juice.
Wash and inspect for sand
and shells:
2 pounds scallops

Put in a saucepan and simmer
for about 5 minutes:
scallops
1/2 cup white wine
1/2 cup water
1 clove garlic, minced fine
2 shallots, minced fine
1/2 teaspoon salt
1/4 teaspoon white pepper
juice from scallops

After cooking, drain off the juice
(*about 2 cups*), and add:
1/2 cup light cream
1/2 teaspoon herb salt

In another saucepan, make a
roux with:
4 tablespoons butter
4 tablespoons flour

Add roux to above liquid and cook
until thick, stirring constantly.
Then add:
2 teaspoons lemon juice

Fold the thickened liquid mixture
with the scallops and add:
4 eggs, hard–boiled, that
    have been quartered
    and then halved

Put the scallop mixture into the
individual casseroles and garnish
on each side with the carrot mixture.
In the middle put 3 small cherry
tomatoes. Bake at 400° until mixture
begins to bubble. Serve immediately.

Serves 4

Deep Fried Scallops with Herb Sauce

Put oil in deep frying pan and heat very hot. Drop in and fry golden brown:

2 pounds breaded scallops, fresh or frozen

Braise in butter:

2/3 cup sliced mushrooms

Put into blender which has been heated with warm water:

4 egg yolks (*at room temperature*)
1 cup melted butter
   (*heated until it begins to boil*)
1/3 cup hot sherry

Start blender whirling the egg yolks, and pour in immediately the wine and butter mixture. Whirl for about 10 seconds.

Add:

above mushrooms
1/2 cup lemon juice
1/2 teaspoon celery seeds
4 sprigs of lemon thyme
1/2 cup parsley
1 teaspoon salt

Run in blender until thoroughly blended.

Serve sauce in small dish for dipping. Rice should accompany this dish.

Serves 6

Swordfish with Bercy Sauce

Prepare 5 pounds of swordfish steak, 3/4–inch thick by laying on each piece a thin slice of butter. Broil until brown. Sprinkle with a little herb salt.

Now add and bake for 20 minutes at 350º:

1 cup white wine
1 teaspoon fish herb blend

Bercy Sauce

Strain off:

1 1/3 fish juice

Combine in pan with:

1 pound of butter

Bring to boil and then, immediately add to:

6 egg yolks (*in warmed blender*)

Blend for 10 seconds, or less until thick, no more.

To serve, place portion of swordfish in casserole and heat in oven to serving temperature. Spoon over it some Bercy sauce, which should be at room temperature. Do not heat sauce in oven as it will separate.

Garnish with minced parsley.

Serves 6

CHICKEN

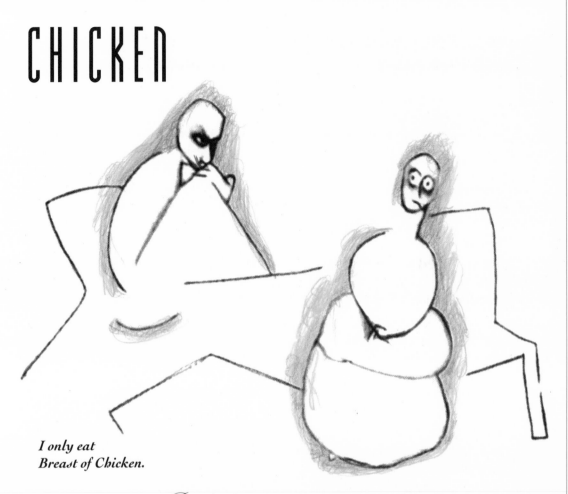

*I only eat
Breast of Chicken.*

*B*ECAUSE SUCH A TREMENDOUS VARIETY OF SEASONINGS CAN BE USED WITH CHICKEN, IT IS SIMPLER TO START OFF WITH THE WARNING THAT THERE ARE A FEW STRONG HERBS, SUCH AS SAGE AND ROSEMARY, THAT ONE SHOULD USE WITH CAUTION. COOKS WHO LIKE TO EX-PERIMENT HAVE A BOUQUET OF FLAVORING COMBINATIONS AT THEIR COMMAND, NEEDING ONLY TO KEEP IN MIND THAT ONE MUST MAINTAIN THE BALANCE OF THE HERBS WHEN USING MORE THAN ONE, SO THAT ONE HERB DOES NOT OVERPOWER ANOTHER.

THE HERBS THAT GO BEST WITH CHICKEN ARE THE MILDER ONES, SUCH AS SWEET MARJORAM, BASIL, THYME, CELERY, ONION, LOVAGE, COSTMARY, PARSLEY, PINEAPPLE SAGE, LEMON VERBENA, A LITTLE LEMON BALM, AND CHERVIL AND SUMMER SAVORY IN MODERATION. ONE CAN USE SWEET THINGS FOR FLAVORING LIKE FRUIT, OR TART THINGS LIKE TOMATOES, VEGETABLES, GREEN PEPPERS AND OLIVES; THEN THERE IS THE WORLD OF WINES TO ENHANCE THESE FLAVORS. CORDIALS AND LIQUEURS ARE EXCELLENT FLAVORING DIVERSIONS FOR THIS ELEGANT MEAT. JUST KEEP IN MIND THAT THE MEAT ITSELF IS OF A DELICATE FLAVOR AND THE LIGHT TOUCH IS INDICATED.

IF YOUR RECIPE CALLS FOR CUTTING THE CHICKEN INTO PIECES FOR BAKING OR FRYING, THE FIRST THING TO DO WITH THE PIECES IS TO BROWN THEM QUICKLY AND LIGHTLY IN BUTTER, OR HALF BUTTER AND HALF PEANUT OR OLIVE OIL, TO SEAL IN THE JUICES. IF NOT TREATED IN THIS WAY, THE CHICKEN CAN BE VERY DRY, ESPECIALLY THE WHITE MEAT.

Chicken Poached
in Champagne

When I began to think about meat dishes to add to our menu after we reopened the Ranch House, the idea of adding the magical taste of champagne to the delicate flavor of chicken intrigued me. I began experimenting, trying various combinations of ingredients and various types of champagne. I found that for cooking, the best champagne to use is an inexpensive, strong-flavored type; such a wine will best impart the exciting champagne flavor to the dish.

Cook until cleared:
**1 onion, minced in
   2 tablespoons butter**

Add and cook 1 minute:
5 mushrooms, sliced

Grind in mortar:
**1 teaspoon salt
4 lemon verbena leaves
3 mint leaves
4 sprigs marjoram
4 sprigs thyme
1/2 cup chopped parsley
1 clove garlic, minced
1/8 teaspoon pepper**

Add herbs to onion mixture
and mix with:
**3/4 cup champagne,
   just uncorked**

The bubbling process of the champagne while mixing imparts extra flavor to the sauce.

Brown lightly in butter:
**2 chickens, cut in
   serving pieces**
   (use no flour)

Lay chicken pieces in pan that can be tightly covered. Pour champagne mixture over chicken and marinate for 4 hours, then simmer *(do not boil)* for 1 hour. Remove chicken and thicken sauce with flour.

Serves 4

Chicken Livers with Spanish Sauce

Make the following Spanish sauce.

Cook in kettle until just done:
2 cups onions, cut coarse
2 cups celery, cut coarse
2 green peppers, cut coarse
1 cup mushrooms, sliced
1 cup peeled, seeded tomatoes
2 vegetable bouillon cubes
1 bay leaf
1 clove garlic, minced
1 teaspoon tomato herb blend
1 small can pimentos, diced
5 green, stuffed olives,
**   cut across**
1/2 cup olive oil

Sauté in olive oil until just done and the livers are no longer bloody:
2 pounds chicken livers,
**   well drained**
4 tablespoons olive oil

When livers are done, add sauce. Allow to marinate for at least 20 minutes to blend flavors.

Serve with:
rice
chopped parsley
paprika

Serves 6

Chicken with Brie

Bone and then stuff with slices of Brie, 1 chicken breast per order. Dust with flour, then beaten egg, and then bread crumbs.

Lay in a baking pan, with 1 cup cream. Cover tightly and bake until just done, about 45 minutes at 375°.

Sauce
Heat in a double boiler:
1 pound Béchamel sauce
    (page 43)
1 pint coffee cream,
**   half and half**
1 teaspoon
**   Worcestershire sauce**
dash herb salt
dash cayenne pepper
1 tablespoon sherry
3/4 pound Brie

Stir with whip until smooth.

Arrange chicken on serving plate, spoon on the sauce and garnish with pimento strips.

Chicken Amaretto

Bake at 425° for 45 minutes:
6 chicken breasts, boned
1/2 cup amaretto
1/2 chopped bell pepper
8 ounces sliced mushrooms

Sprinkle with:
herb salt
almonds, chopped
    and slivered
coconut

Sauce
Drain pan juice, then add:
2 cups whipping cream
2 egg yolks
pinch starch (about 1 ounce)
    and water
2 ounces amaretto
3 leaves sorrel (pounded in
    1/4 teaspoon herb salt)
1/2 teaspoon herb salt
1/8 teaspoon nutmeg

Cook until thick, then spoon sauce over chicken breasts and top with sliced almonds, toasted.

Serves 6

Chicken St. Moritz

Fry until lightly brown:
8 chicken breasts in
    half butter,
    half peanut oil

Sauté in saucepan until just done:
4 tablespoons olive oil
4 tablespoons butter
4 large onions, minced

Then add and simmer until thick:
3 pounds tomatoes,
    skinned and seeded
2 tablespoons thyme
3 ounces sherry
1/2 teaspoon salt
1/4 teaspoon pepper

Place mixture on browned chicken breasts and sprinkle with grated Gruyere cheese and a small amount of cream. Bake in covered baking pan 35 to 40 minutes, or until done, in a 400° oven.

Serves 8

Stuffed Quail with Pomegranate & Madeira

Bring the following to a boil and
reduce by half:
1 1/4 cups pomegranate juice
1 cup beef stock
1/2 cup Madeira wine
1/2 cup brandy
1/4 cup orange juice
2 cloves garlic, crushed
2 sprigs of thyme
10 juniper berries, crushed
3 peppercorns, cracked

When reduced, strain sauce and
thicken with:
3 or 4 tablespoons cornstarch

Stuff the quail, 2 per serving, with
apple and date stuffing (*page 125*).
Brush sauce on birds and broil
breast side up 3 or 4 minutes. Serve
hot with small amount of sauce
over bird.

Garnish with:
slice of apple
parsley

*The eight o'clock
reservation.*

Walnut Chicken
with Chutney Glaze

Use a boneless breast of chicken that has had the skin and any extra fat removed. Pound with a mallet until a uniform thickness has been attained – you will want it fairly thin, but do not tear. Mold the following dressing into a cylinder, place on each breast, and roll the breast up.

Place in baking dish that has been brushed with butter and brush the top of the chicken roll with butter. Bake in a preheated 400° oven approximately 20 minutes depending on the size of the roll.

Serve on a bed of griced spinach and top with a small ladle of the glaze. Garnish with orange slices if desired.

Dressing

Sauté until tender, but do not overcook:
3 ounces butter
1 small onion, minced
2 ribs celery, minced
1 tablespoon garlic, minced

Add the rest of the following and check for moistness. If toodry, add more melted butter or a small amount of chicken broth:

1 cup walnuts, toasted and chopped coarse
2 cups breadcrumbs, mixed white and wheat
1 teaspoon salt
1/4 teaspoon black pepper
1/8 teaspoon powdered cloves
1/8 teaspoon cinnamon
1 teaspoon sage

Glaze

Put in a heavy saucepan and boil until it starts to color and thicken:
4 cups white vinegar
2 cups sugar

Add and continue to simmer for 10 minutes:
1 cup orange juice

Stir in and remove from heat:
3/4 cup chutney, run through the blender

Boneless thighs may also be used. You will probably have to use 2 to an order, placing the dressing between the thighs and securing it with string. Baking time will vary depending upon the thickness of the chicken. Be sure to remove the string before serving.

Serves 8

Coconut Chicken with Curry

Remove the skin from 3 whole chicken breasts and cut the meat into bite-sized pieces. Marinate the chicken in the marinade for at least 2 hours.

For the marinade combine:
1 cup tamari or soy sauce
1/2 cup pineapple juice
3 cloves garlic, minced
1 ounce peanut oil
1 ounce curry powder
1 ounce brown sugar

When ready to serve, remove chicken pieces from marinade and sauté in peanut oil until just done. Marinade can be reused.

Sauce for Chicken

Sauté until clear:
1 ounce peanut oil
1 onion, chopped
5 cloves garlic, minced

Add and sauté briefly:
1/4 cup curry powder

Now add:
8 ounces almond butter
6 ounces pineapple juice
3 tablespoons tamari or
    soy sauce
1 tablespoon brown sugar
2 14-ounce cans coconut milk

Put above ingredients into blender and whirl until sauce is smooth. You can heat the sauce and warm the chicken in it if you wish to sauté the chicken ahead of time. Serve on a bed of rice and garnish with chutney and fresh grated coconut.

Serves 8

Chicken Tahitian

Bring to a boil:
1 cup coconut milk
1 1/2 teaspoons curry powder
1/3 teaspoon nutmeg
1 tablespoon lemon juice
3/4 teaspoon herb salt
4 tablespoons apricot jam

Thicken with:
**flour and water until
    consistency of gravy**

Now add and stir in:
1/2 cup sour cream
2 cups Béchamel sauce (*page 43*)

Prepare chicken legs (*3 per person*) by cutting the tendons at foot end of bone. Draw out bone.

Sprinkle with lemon juice and a little herb salt:
King crab leg meat
    (*1/2 per chicken leg*)

Stuff 1/2 crab leg into chicken leg. Brush with melted butter and broil, not too close to the heat, until done, about 8 minutes on each side.

Serve hot with the above sauce. Garnished with:
freshly grated coconut
slices of fresh lime

Chicken Mandarin

Cut into serving pieces:
2 chickens

Mix together:
1/2 cup flour
1 teaspoon salt
1/4 teaspoon black pepper

Put flour mixture and chicken pieces into paper bag and shake until chicken is well coated with flour. Brown chicken in:
butter

Remove chicken to shallow baking pan that can be tightly covered.

Mix together and pour over chicken:
**juice from 1 11–ounce can
    Mandarin oranges**
1/3 cup Kikkoman soy sauce
**1/4 cup firmly packed
    brown sugar**
1/2 teaspoon mace

Bake chicken at 350° for 40 minutes, basting twice with sauce from pan. Remove from oven, baste with sauce and arrange over chicken:
Mandarin orange pieces

Return to oven and bake 20 minutes longer. Serve hot with rice.

Serves 6

Chicken Cerise

Cut into serving pieces:
4 chickens

Fry until lightly brown in:
half butter, half peanut oil

Lay pieces in pan that can be tightly covered and sprinkle lightly with:
herb salt

Mix together then pour around the edges of the pan, so that the herb salt will not be washed off:
**juice from 1 28–ounce can
    dark sweet cherries**
1/2 cup Cherry Kijafa wine
4 tablespoons lemon juice
4 drops red food coloring
    (*only 4*)

Cover pan and bake at 400º until done, about 40 to 45 minutes. Drain juice and skim fat from it. Taste juice for tartness; it may need a little more lemon juice. Boil gently until reduced by half.

Adjust seasoning by adding:
chicken base concentrate

Dissolve in a little water and stir in:
2 tablespoons cornstarch

When thickened, add cherries and serve over chicken pieces.

Serves 8

Chicken Romanoff

Cheese Sauce

Prepare cheese sauce by heating in double boiler:
1 1/4 cups Béchamel sauce
    (*page 43*)
1 1/4 cups coffee cream
**1 cup very sharp Cheddar
    cheese, grated**
**1/2 teaspoon
    Worcestershire sauce**
dash herb salt
dash cayenne pepper
    (*not too much*)
1/2 tablespoon sherry

Place in baking dish or pan:
**8 servings of cooked chicken
    or turkey slices**

Sprinkle with herb salt.

Place on each serving, cut side down:
**1/2 cooked broccoli spear,
    cut lengthwise**

Top with:
cheese sauce

Bake at 350º until sauce begins to bubble. Garnish with:
minced parsley
paprika

Serves 8

Chicken Soubise

Cut into serving pieces:
2 chickens

Fry until lightly brown in:
half butter, half peanut oil

Lay pieces in pan that can be tightly covered. Lay over the chicken:
**1/2 cup onion, sliced
   paper thin**

Sprinkle on:
**1/2 cup mushrooms,
   chopped fine
herb salt** (lightly)

Pour around sides of pan:
1/4 cup white wine

Cover pan and bake at 400° until done, about 40 minutes. Drain and reserve liquid.

Sauce Soubise

1 cup onions, sliced very thin

Cook onions for
10 minutes (no more) in:
rich beef stock (can be made
   by mixing 1 teaspoon beef base
   in 1/2 cup water)

Drain onions and discard liquid. Add to drained onions and cook slowly for 5 minutes without browning, as this is to be a white sauce:
**1 tablespoon butter
1/2 teaspoon herb salt**

Mix together and add to onions, stirring well:
**1/2 cup cheese sauce
liquid from chicken** (enough to
   give the sauce a proper consistency)

Serve sauce over chicken.
Garnish with:
**watercress
paprika**

Serves 4

Chicken Toledo

Cut into serving pieces:
2 chickens

Fry until lightly brown in:
olive oil

Lay pieces in pan that can be tightly covered. Sprinkle with:
herb salt

Spread over chicken:
**1 small onion, sliced
    paper thin**

Mix together and spread over the above:
**1 large green pepper, cubed
1/2 can pitted ripe olives,
    cut into fourths
1/2 can pitted green olives,
    cut into fourths
1 small can pimentos, cubed**

Sprinkle on:
1 teaspoon meat herb blend

Pour around sides of pan so as not to disturb olive mixture:
1/4 cup dry white wine

Cover tightly and bake at 375° until done, about 1 hour. Drain off liquid and skim excess fat. Thicken liquid with:
**2 tablespoons flour,
    dissolved in a little water**

Add to thickened gravy:
**olives from pan
1/2 can pitted ripe olives,
    sliced into fourths
1/2 can pitted green olives,
    sliced into fourths**

Spoon gravy over chicken servings.

Serves 6

Chicken Bombay

Heat in large frying pan:
4 tablespoons butter

Add and fry until light brown:
**4 chickens, cut up into
    serving pieces**

Cook until clear:
2 onions, minced
2 cloves garlic, minced
2 tablespoons butter

Add, and continue to cook until
mushy, on very low heat:
4 tablespoons curry powder

Add and cook slowly for 15 minutes:
1/2 cup fresh coconut milk

Add and reheat:
3/4 cup sour cream
1/4 cup orange marmalade
**4 vegetable cubes, or
    chicken bouillon cubes**

Dip fried chicken in this curry
mixture and lay in baking pan.
Add to remaining curry mixture:
2 cups chicken or turkey stock

Add to remaining butter in chicken
frying pan, and fry until light brown:
1/2 cup coarse grated coconut

Add curry mixture to browned
coconut and mix together well. Pour
over the chicken in baking pan.

Slice thin and then cut in half:
2 lemons or limes

Lay these on pieces of chicken in
pan. Cover tightly and bake at 400°
for about 45 minutes or until done.
Drain off juice and thicken it slightly.
Serve with pieces of the baked lemon
on each portion, using juice.

Serves 8 to 10

Chicken Aloha

Melt in a saucepan that can be later heated over water:
1/4 pound butter

Add and braise 5 minutes:
1 clove garlic, minced
4 green onions and tops, cut up
4 ounces fresh mushrooms, sliced

Add and mix well:
3 tablespoons flour
1 teaspoon salt

Add, cook and stir until thick:
1 cup Chablis or any white wine
1 tablespoon lemon juice

Add and heat over water:
1/3 cup canned bamboo shoots, sliced
1/3 cup canned water chestnuts, sliced

1 cup canned pineapple bits, drained
1/2 cup juice from canned pineapple
1/4 cup blanched almonds, toasted lightly
1 tablespoon frozen orange juice concentrate
1 1/2 tablespoons honey

When hot, add and mix gently:
1 1/2 pounds cooked chicken, diced
herb salt

Serve over rice, garnished with:
macadamia nuts

Serves 6

I asked for the recipe.

Chicken Vermouth

Nancy Adams, our hostess for many years at the Ranch House, gave me this recipe and told me a little story about it which I shall pass along for those who may feel some hesitation about entering the world of gourmet cookery.

"Sometimes, psychologically speaking," Nancy said, "we take a giant step in life. My mother was a fabulous cook; my sister, apparently with the greatest ease, became a fabulous cook. I observed all this with awe, helped set the table, entertained our guests, enjoyed the delicious food — and was secretly frightened at the thought of trying to understand all those kitchen mysteries. I thought good food must come from complicated recipes and take great skill to concoct. I felt I just wasn't that intelligent. Cooking wasn't my thing; if I tried, it could only end in disaster."

Nancy came West and went to visit a family friend in San Francisco. The friend took her sightseeing and shopping, and around 5 o'clock in the afternoon they stopped at a market to get food for dinner, including a chicken. At home, her hostess spent a few minutes in the kitchen; then they had a drink and a little before 6 the husband came home. They had another drink and her friend went to the kitchen for another half hour or so.

"In no time at all after that," said Nancy, "we sat down to a dinner that tasted as though she had spent all day in the kitchen. If food that good could be that easily prepared, perhaps even I could cook. I asked for the recipe, tried it, and it was a success. I had taken my giant step, and have been cooking like mad ever since."

Rub:
6 breasts of chicken with garlic

Sprinkle with:
fresh lime juice

Let stand for at least half an hour. Dip chicken pieces in:
melted butter

Put pieces in baking pan and sprinkle with:
herb salt

Add to melted butter and pour over chicken:
1/2 cup dry vermouth

Bake 1 hour at 350°, turning and basting every 15 minutes. Brown under broiler for a few minutes before serving.

Serves 4

Chicken Curaçao

Have the butcher quarter:
4 chickens

Brush chicken pieces lightly
with:
melted butter

Broil until golden brown, then
place in tightly covered baking
pan and bake at 400° until tender,
about 30 minutes.

To make sauce, mix together:
1 cup orange juice
1 teaspoon minced
orange rind
   (cut off rind very thin, using
   none of the white part)
1 cup white Karo syrup
1/4 teaspoon cardamom,
powdered
1 tablespoon butter
2 tablespoons brown sugar
1 tablespoon cornstarch,
dissolved in a little water

Cook until thickened, then add and
boil gently for 5 minutes:
1 orange, scrubbed and sliced
into 8 slices

When done add:
1/3 cup Curaçao liquor

Remove orange slices and put aside
to garnish chicken. Brush chicken
pieces again lightly with melted
butter and put under broiler until
they sizzle, then plunge them in
very hot sauce for about 10 minutes.
Use an orange slice for each serving.

Serves 8

Chicken Paprikash

Cut into serving pieces:
1 chicken

Mix together:
1/2 cup white flour
1 teaspoon paprika
1/2 teaspoon salt
1/4 teaspoon white pepper

Put the flour mixture into a paper bag and shake the chicken pieces, a few at a time, to coat them.

Melt in a skillet:
2 tablespoons butter

Brown chicken pieces in the butter and remove them. Add to skillet and cook 3 minutes:
1 onion, minced
2 tablespoons butter

Put chicken back in pan and add:
1 tablespoon paprika
1/2 cup water poured around, not over, the chicken

Cover and cook for 45 minutes. Turn the chicken pieces as necessary to keep them from sticking. If needed, add a small amount of warm water. Remove chicken when done and add to pan gravy, mixing well:
2 tablespoons flour

When gravy is smooth, add:
2 cups sour cream

Cook gently until thick, then add chicken pieces and simmer slowly for another 5 minutes to blend flavors. Serve with rice or peasant noodles.

Serves 4

Chicken Hungarian

Cut into serving pieces:
4 chickens

Mix together:
1 cup white flour
2 teaspoons salt
1 teaspoon black pepper
4 teaspoons paprika

Coat chicken pieces with flour mixture and fry to golden red–brown in:
half butter, half olive oil

Place chicken pieces in pan with tight cover.

Sauce

Sauté until nearly done:
4 tablespoons olive oil
2 cloves garlic, minced
1 large onion, sliced thin

Add and cook for 3 minutes:
2 green peppers, chopped coarse
1/2 teaspoon basil
1 tablespoon cilantro
1 cup chicken stock

Spoon sauce over chicken.
Pour around edges of pan:
1 1/2 cups red wine

Cover tightly and bake at 400° until done, about 45 minutes. Drain liquid from chicken and skim well, then stir in:
1 teaspoon paprika
1 teaspoon chicken base
**2 tablespoons cornstarch
   mixed in a little water**

When sauce is thick, add and stir in well:
1 cup sour cream

To serve, spoon sauce over chicken pieces and garnish with sour cream.

Serves 8

Chicken Calavo

Combine in a saucepan:
4 tablespoons butter
4 tablespoons flour
1/2 teaspoon herb salt

Add and stir over low heat
until thick:
1 1/2 cups milk
1 cup cream or
evaporated milk

Add and mix lightly:
1 tablespoon sherry
1 pound cooked chicken,
diced large
1/2 teaspoon herb salt
1/2 teaspoon salt

Cut lengthwise, pit and peel:
avocados to cover
bottom of casserole

Lay avocado halves in casserole,
pit side up, and spoon the chicken
mixture over them. Sprinkle lightly
with:
Cheddar cheese, grated

Bake at 400° until edges of sauce
start to bubble. Do not overcook, as
avocados tend to develop an acid
taste when overcooked.

Serves 6

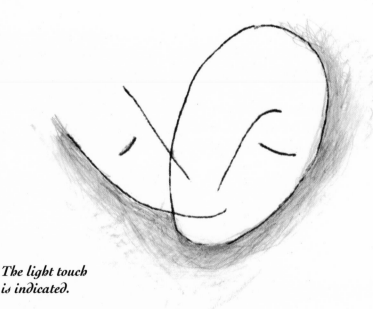

*The light touch
is indicated.*

Chicken Cacciatore

This is the second of the three attractive names of meat dishes I decided to add to our menu as we began to serve meat. I went about the concocting of the dish much as I had done with the stroganoff, and here is the recipe as we now serve it.

Cook until cleared:
1 large onion, chopped fine
2 cloves garlic, chopped fine
2 tablespoons olive oil

Add and cook for 30 minutes:
1 16–ounce can Italian–style
   (*pear*) **tomatoes**
1 teaspoon salt
dash black pepper
1 bay leaf (*discard when cooked*)
2 sprigs thyme
1 sprig basil
2 sprigs oregano
pinch rosemary
pinch summer savory
1/2 cup sliced mushrooms
4 tablespoons tomato paste
   (*optional*)

Lower heat and mash tomatoes. Simmer 4 hours, adding:
3 tablespoons dry Burgundy

Dust with flour and brown in olive oil:
4 frying chickens, jointed

Place chicken in Dutch oven–type cooker and add enough sauce to cover it. Do not use too much sauce, just enough for each piece. A few tablespoons of water in the bottom of the cooker will prevent sticking. Simmer 45 minutes or until chicken is done.

Serve with:
vermicelli or other type pasta
grated Parmesan cheese

Serves 8

Chicken Tetrazzini

Cook and strain:
1 3/4 cups chicken broth
1 1/2 cups celery, chopped fine
1/2 cup onion, chopped fine
1/2 cup parsley
1 sprig marjoram
1 sprig thyme
1 small bay leaf
   (discard when cooked)

Sauté:
3/4 pound fresh mushrooms,
   cut coarse
4 tablespoons butter

In top of large double boiler put:
1 1/2 cups of above
   strained broth
1 1/2 cups coffee cream or
   evaporated milk

Heat and thicken with:
3/8 cup flour, dissolved in
   a little water
2 1/4 teaspoons salt
1/4 teaspoon fresh–ground
   black pepper
1/4 teaspoon garlic salt

Add mushrooms and:
2 1/2 pounds diced,
   cooked chicken
3 tablespoons sherry

Heat over water. Place in small casseroles over cooked noodles, spaghetti or other pasta, top with grated Parmesan cheese and bread crumbs, and brown slightly under broiler.

Serves 8

Cannelloni with Chicken

Prepare the chicken filling as you would for chicken tetrazzini except that the mushrooms are optional and usually omitted. Use less sherry – a thin sauce will run out of the noodles.

Prepare cannelloni noodles as directed on package. Lay flat on a board and fill one end of the rectangle. Fold over to make long cylinders and place in shallow baking pan. Spoon some of the chicken sauce over them and top with a generous sprinkling of Parmesan cheese.

Bake at about 350° until the sauce begins to bubble around the edges. Have enough sauce so that they will not dry out.

A little dry white wine is sometimes added at the edge of the pan to moisten and heighten the flavor. Serve on hot plates.

Serves 8 or more

Chicken Enchiladas with Guacamole & Sour Cream

When you are cooking chickens and do not need to use the necks, backs and wings, freeze these pieces to be used later to make this delicious dish.

Boil for 30 minutes in a covered pan, using very little water:
**necks, backs and wings from
    2 chickens**

Drain broth and reserve for other uses.

Remove meat from bones and cut into small pieces.

Make and mix with the chicken:
**1 cup rich cream sauce or
    Béchamel sauce** (*page 43*)

Do not make the mixture mushy.

Put in blender and blend thoroughly:
**2 peeled and halved avocados
1 cup sour cream
1 sprig cilantro
1/2 teaspoon herb salt**

Pour avocado mixture into shallow pan or bowl.

Heat so that they will bend easily:
8 tortillas (*must be fresh*)

Put the chicken mixture on each tortilla, roll it up, and dip it into the avocado sauce mixture. Lay the rolls in a pan and heat in the oven to serving temperature. Serve topped with sour cream.

Serves 4

Chicken Verde

Cut into serving pieces:
2 chickens

Fry until lightly brown in:
half butter, half olive oil

Lay pieces in pan that can be tightly covered and sprinkle lightly with:
herb salt

Mix together:
**6 green onions, cut diagonally
    into 1–inch pieces
2 garlic cloves, chopped fine
1 green pepper, cut in long
    thin strips
1/4 cup chopped parsley
1 green chili, minced**
    (canned will do)
**1/4 teaspoon basil
1/4 teaspoon marjoram
1/2 teaspoon cilantro**

Heat in frying pan until almost smoking:
1/4 cup olive oil

Add chopped vegetables to oil and cook until just tender but not quite done, then add:
**1 teaspoon herb salt
1 pound fresh, or 1 small can
    tomatillos** *(fresh tomatillos are
    nearly always available in a good
    Mexican market)*

Mix vegetables together and spoon over chicken pieces. Cover tightly and bake at 400° until done, about 45 minutes.

Drain off liquid and skim fat. Thicken gravy slightly with flour and serve over chicken.

Serves 6

*I'm mad about
Mexican food.*

Chicken Helene

In the late '20s, toward the end of that era, I was with a jazz band, playing in a nightclub outside Milwaukee. Nowadays kitchens of nightclubs seem to specialize in beef, but the famed specialty of this Milwaukee club was chicken — fried chicken and chicken livers. The chef was a slight, always tired-looking woman named Helene. Her chicken soup was also much in demand, and she had another popular dish which she called gizzard stew. She let me have the recipes, and I think you will enjoy them.

To prepare chickens for 4 (*or any multiple of this*), cut into serving pieces:
2 chickens

Put the pieces in a pot, just cover with water and boil until nearly but not quite done. Drain and refrigerate the chicken pieces until very cold. Reserve the broth for soup.

In a Dutch oven or heavy iron pot with a lid, heat to 375°:
half butter, half vegetable oil, to a depth of 2 or 3 inches
(*deeper for more chicken*)

Dip cold chicken pieces in:
French–frying batter with 1 extra egg

Put the chicken into the hot fat, cover and fry until golden brown. The butter will go into the batter for flavor and the vegetable oil will keep the butter from burning or browning the chicken too fast. The cover causes the chicken to steam so that it is done all the way through. If these directions are followed exactly, you will have fried chicken with a flavor you may never have tasted before.

Batter for French-Frying Vegetables

Mix well together:
2 eggs
1/4 cup water
1/4 cup Kikkoman soy sauce
3/4 cup white flour

Coat cubed assorted vegetables with this mixture and fry in deep fat. When golden brown, drain on paper towels and keep warm until ready to serve.

Chef Helene's Chicken Livers Espagnole

Put into kettle that can be covered and cook until clear:
1/4 cup olive oil
2 cloves garlic, minced

Mix together and add to garlic:
4 stalks celery, cut coarse
2 onions, cut coarse
1/4 cup parsley, chopped fine
1/2 teaspoon basil
1/2 teaspoon marjoram
1/4 teaspoon thyme
1/4 teaspoon pepper
2 teaspoons herb salt

When onions and celery are just done but not mushy, add and bring to boil:
1 28-ounce can tomatoes, mashed
3 pimentos, chopped
1 teaspoon lemon or lime juice
2 cups mushrooms, sliced

Bring to high heat in a skillet:
4 tablespoons chicken fat or butter (*the fat can be heated higher than the butter before burning*)

Add and stir until they are well braised:
2 pounds chicken livers

When livers are cooked to taste, add the sauce and mix in well. Keep warm on low heat until flavors blend, at least 10 minutes. Serve with rice to which has been added a dash of saffron or turmeric. This makes a fine luncheon dish served with a tossed green salad.

Serves 8

Gizzard Stew

Have your butcher reserve for you:
2 pounds chicken gizzards
1 pound hearts and necks

Put giblets into pressure cooker or large pot with:
2 cups water
1/2 teaspoon meat herb blend

Cook at 15 pounds pressure for 30 minutes (*or covered until tender if pot is used*); then drain and reserve broth.

Into another pot put:
1 cup carrots, cut into
**   1-inch pieces**
1 cup celery, cut very coarse
1 cup onions, cut coarse
1/4 cup parsley, chopped
1 cup potatoes, diced large
broth from gizzards

Cook vegetables until just done, add enough extra water to make a stew, then add and cook until thickened:
2 tablespoons flour, mixed in
**   a little water**

Add and mix well:
1/2 teaspoon lemon juice
gizzards that have been
**   cut in half**

Serve in a large tureen, and ladle into bowls. The stew should be juicy to make it enjoyable. Boiled noodles mixed with cooked sliced onions and plenty of butter can be served with this stew.

Serves 8

Chicken Livers & Mushrooms

Wash thoroughly and take out any small parts of gall bladder to avoid bitterness:
1 pound chicken livers with
**   skin intact** (*do not use frozen*)

Braise livers in:
2 tablespoons butter or
**   chicken fat**

Add:
4 ounces mushrooms, sliced
1/2 teaspoon herb salt
1/4 teaspoon meat herb blend
4 tablespoons chicken stock
1 teaspoon chicken base
**   or concentrate**
2 tablespoons Chablis or
**   other white wine**

Cover and cook 10 minutes.

Thicken liquid with:
**2 tablespoons flour,
     mixed in a little water**

Add and stir gently:
1/2 teaspoon lemon juice

Serve in casserole over rice.

Serves 4

Chicken Curry

Cook until clear:
**1 onion, minced very fine
2 cloves garlic, minced fine
4 tablespoons butter**

Add and mix in well:
3 1/2 teaspoons curry powder

Simmer for at least 5 minutes on
very low heat (*10 minutes is even better*).

Add and blend in well:
**2 chicken bouillon cubes
1/4 teaspoon salt**

Mix with a little water and stir
in well:
4 tablespoons flour

When thoroughly mixed, add
and cook until thickened:
2 cups milk

Add and stir in well:
**2 tablespoons lemon juice
3 tablespoons apricot jam
     or currant jelly
1 tablespoon sherry**

Add and mix in gently:
3 cups cooked, diced chicken

Sprinkle with:
herb salt

Reheat in double boiler. Serve
with rice to which has been added
a dash of saffron.

Serves 4

Chicken Livers with Allspice

Braise until nearly done, about 3 minutes:
1 pound washed chicken livers
1 small onion, sliced very thin
2 tablespoons butter

Add and continue to cook slowly for about 10 minutes:
1 cup chicken broth, or
   1 chicken bouillon cube
   in 1 cup water
1/2 teaspoon salt (*salt to taste only, if cube is used*)
1/2 teaspoon allspice
1 teaspoon brown sugar
1/2 teaspoon lemon juice

When done, add and cook only until thick:
1 tablespoon cornstarch,
   dissolved in a little water

Serve over rice to which has been added a dash of saffron or turmeric.

Garnish with:
minced parsley
chopped pimentos

Serves 4

Chicken, Shrimp or Crab Gumbo

Put in large kettle with tight lid and boil for 15 minutes:
1 cup water or chicken stock
1 1/2 cups celery, cut coarse
1 cup onions, cut coarse
1/4 cup parsley, chopped fine
1/2 teaspoon salt
1 tablespoon sugar
1/4 teaspoon fresh-ground
   black pepper (*more can be used; in the South it is made very hot*)
4 bay leaves (*discard when cooked*)
4 chicken bouillon cubes

Add and boil for 5 minutes:
1/2 of 16-ounce can tomatoes, mashed

Add and cook to thicken:
2 1/2 tablespoons cornstarch,
   dissolved in a little water

Add and reheat but do not boil:
1 8-ounce can cut okra drained,
   or 1 cup fresh, cooked okra
1 1/2 pounds cooked, diced chicken or fish
1/4 pound cooked, diced ham
   (*very essential for flavor*)

Add and stir in gently, sprinkling over the mixture and stirring in quickly after all other ingredients are added and the mixture is still hot:
1 tablespoon gumbo filé

Do not try to mix the gumbo filé in water first, for it will not dissolve in the gumbo but will make a nasty grey-green paste.

Serves 8

Chicken Teriyaki

Remembering my interest in unusual dishes, my friend Tom Blackburn, after a sojourn in Hawaii, brought back with him a recipe for preparing chicken and other meats which is typical of Island cooking — a marinade of herbs, ginger and white wine. I added a few touches and came up with this recipe which seems to continue in popularity.

Cut in serving pieces, dust with flour and fry lightly in oil:
2 frying chickens

Grind in mortar:
3 tablespoons sugar
1 teaspoon ginger (*ground or fresh*)
2 cloves garlic
3 leaves lemon verbena

Add herbs to:
3/4 cup soy sauce
3/4 cup white wine

Place chicken in roasting dish, pour sauce over it and marinate for 3 hours. Add as a layer over marinated chicken:
8 slices fresh pineapple (*optional*)

Sprinkle with:
2/3 cup brown sugar

Cover, roast in 325° oven for 1 hour. Remove chicken and thicken sauce with starch. Serve with rice.

Serves 6

Chicken in Chablis

Mix together:
1/2 cup flour
1 teaspoon salt
**1/2 teaspoon fresh
    ground pepper**
1 teaspoon paprika

Dip in this dry mixture and fry
in butter until golden brown:
15 chicken pieces

Pound in mortar:
1/4 teaspoon salt
2 cloves garlic
5 sprigs marjoram
5 sprigs mint leaves
2 sprigs summer savory
1/4 teaspoon sage
3 sprigs rosemary
1/2 cup parsley, minced

Braise:
1 tablespoon butter
1 small onion, minced
1/2 clove garlic, minced

Mix onion and garlic with herbs,
then add:
**1 cup Chablis, or other good
    white wine**

Put chicken in shallow dish which
can be tightly covered, and pour
over it the herb and wine mixture.
Bake for 1 hour at 400°. Pour off juice
and thicken it, adding a little water
if necessary. Spoon gravy over
each serving.

Serves 5

Chicken à la King

Heat in double boiler:
1 cup chicken broth
3/4 cup milk
**3/4 cup coffee cream or
    evaporated milk**
1 bay leaf (*remove when
    milk is hot*)
herb salt
dash pepper

Thicken with:
**6 tablespoons flour
    dissolved in water**

Add and mix gently:
5 ounces mushrooms
    (*sautéed in chicken fat or butter*)
**1 1/2 pounds cooked chicken
    or turkey, cut coarse and
    salted lightly with herb salt**
3 tablespoons sherry
**1 1/2 hard boiled eggs, cut
    coarse** (*optional*)

Serve on toast points.

Serves 6

Chicken à la Martha

Cut in pieces:
2 chickens

Rub pieces with:
oil

Sprinkle with:
tarragon
herb salt
pepper

Lay in greased baking pan and
bake 1 hour at 350º.

Sauté in butter:
2 green peppers, chopped
2 onions, chopped fine
4 ounces mushrooms

Remove from stove and add:
4 ounces pineapple chunks
and a little juice
1 cup dry Sauterne
1 1/2 tablespoons starch
dissolved in water

Cook to thicken slightly.

Place chicken on bed of rice and
pour sauce over it. Garnish with
slivered almonds that have been
fried crisp in butter.

Serves 6

*Then there is
the world of wines
to enhance
these flavors.*

Chicken Creole

Cut into serving pieces:
5 chickens

Mix together:
1 cup flour
2 teaspoons salt
1 teaspoon pepper
2 teaspoons paprika

Dip chicken pieces in the seasoned flour and fry until golden brown.

Prepare these vegetables:
4 onions, cut coarse
6 stalks celery, cut coarse
2 cloves garlic, minced
4 large green peppers,
   cut coarse

Put in pan:
4 tablespoons butter
2 tablespoons water

Add vegetables in layers, celery first, then onions and garlic, then peppers. This keeps peppers from overcooking. Cook until vegetables are just beginning to get done but not soft.

Mix together and cook for about 10 minutes:
1 pint chicken stock
1/2 cup white wine
1/2 cup tomato juice
1 bay leaf
1/2 cup chopped parsley
2 small cans pimentos,
   cut coarse
1/16 teaspoon nutmeg
1/16 teaspoon powdered cloves
1/8 teaspoon thyme leaves,
   whole
2 tablespoons chicken base, or
   4 chicken bouillon cubes
2 1/2 tablespoons lemon juice
1/2 teaspoon fresh ground
   black pepper

Put chicken pieces in covered baking pan, add vegetables, spoon sauce over them and bake at 375° for 1 hour.

When ready to serve, drain juice and thicken it if necessary. Serve chicken with vegetables still lying over it, and spoon sauce over each serving.

Serve with Southern–style cooked rice in generous portions.

Serves 10

Chicken Provençal

Have cut up:
2 chickens

Mix together and dip chicken pieces in:
1 cup flour
2 teaspoons salt
**1 teaspoon fresh ground
    black pepper**
2 teaspoons paprika

Fry golden brown in equal parts of:
butter and peanut oil

Place pieces in shallow baking pan and pour over it:
**3/4 cup Chablis, or other
    good white wine**

Cover tightly and bake at 400° for about 1 hour, or until done.

Drain chicken, leaving a small amount to keep chicken from drying out.

Sauté:
1 tablespoon butter
1 small onion, chopped fine
**1/2 cup fresh mushrooms,
    chopped fine**

Add:
liquid from chicken
**7 ounces coffee cream or
    evaporated milk**
1 cup chicken broth
1/2 teaspoon herb salt
1/2 teaspoon curry powder
**1/2 teaspoon chicken
    herb blend**

Thicken with:
**2 tablespoons flour, dissolved
    in a little water**

Then add:
1 tablespoon lemon juice

Serve over chicken.

Serves 4

Pollo Arandano

Use a boneless breast of chicken that has had the skin and any extra fat removed. Pound with a mallet until a uniform thickness has been attained – you will want it fairly thin, but do not tear. Mold the following dressing into a cylinder and place on each breast and roll the breast up. Place in baking dish that has been brushed with butter and brush the top of the chicken roll with butter. Bake in a preheated 400° oven approximately 20 minutes depending on the size of the roll. Serve on a bed of griced spinach and top with a small ladle of the glaze.

Dressing

Sauté until tender, but do not overcook:
1/2 cup walnut oil
1 1/2 onions, minced
4 ribs celery, minced
2 tablespoons garlic, minced

Add the following and check for moistness. If too dry, add some melted butter or a small amount of chicken broth:
1 cup dried cranberries
2 cups wild rice, cooked
1 teaspoon salt
1 teaspoon thyme
2 cups Wild Boar sausage, cooked and minced

Glaze

Put in a heavy saucepan and boil for 10 minutes:
1/2 cup sugar
1/2 cup water
6 ounces cranberries

Run cranberry mixture in blender until puréed with:
1/4 cup Tequila

In a saucepan add and cook until slightly thick and brown:
3/4 cup water
3/4 cup vinegar
1 1/2 cups sugar

Remove from heat and stir in:
cranberry and Tequila mixture

Serve over stuffed chicken breasts.

BEEF

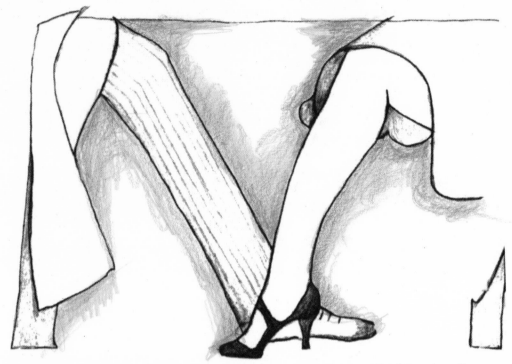

Beef Stroganoff.

$\mathcal{A}$ FEW YEARS AGO I WAS BEING TAKEN AROUND ROME
BY A FRIEND TO ONE RESTAURANT AFTER ANOTHER. THERE WERE
NO STEAK HOUSES SUCH AS WE HAVE IN THIS COUNTRY AND I
SAID TO HER, "I AM GOING TO COME OVER HERE AND OPEN A
STEAK HOUSE."

"WHERE," SHE SAID, "WILL YOU GET THE STEAK? THERE
IS NO AGED BEEF IN ROME THAT I KNOW ANYTHING ABOUT."

THAT WAS SOME YEARS AGO AND THINGS MAY HAVE
CHANGED, BUT GENERALLY IN EUROPE THE FAVORITE MEAT OF
THE BOVINE ANIMAL IS YOUNG, TENDER WHITE VEAL, WHICH

WE ARE NOT SO ACCUSTOMED TO IN THIS COUNTRY. THOUGH IN BRITAIN BEEF IS STANDARD ON THE MENU, IT IS NOT AGED TO OUR TASTE, AND IS THEREFORE APT TO BE TOUGH AND IS CUSTOMARILY SLICED VERY THIN IN SERVING. SO, IN AN AMERICAN RESTAURANT WE ASK FOR AN ENGLISH CUT IF WE WANT THIN SLICES OF ROAST BEEF, AND FOR A DIAMOND JIM BRADY CUT IF WE WANT AN EXTRA THICK SLICE.

BEEF IS A STRONG-FLAVORED MEAT SO ONE OF THE BEST HERBS TO GO ALONG WITH IT IS BAY LEAF. BLACK PEPPER AND HORSERADISH ARE ALSO FAVORITES OF LONG STANDING. (WHAT BRITISH HOUSEWIFE WOULD SERVE BOILED BEEF WITHOUT ITS ACCOMPANYING HORSERADISH!) A MIXTURE SUCH AS OUR OWN HERB BLEND FOR MEAT IS ACCEPTABLE, AND OF COURSE CHIVES AND GARLIC ARE LIKED BY ALMOST EVERYONE. MANY BEEF EATERS DO NOT WANT ANYTHING AT ALL ON THEIR BEEF, THEY SO MUCH LIKE ITS FLAVOR AU NATUREL.

Tournedos Béarnaise

The tournedos is the finest cut of beef – an 8-inch piece of the center of the tenderloin strip is used. The cuts are usually 1/2 to 3/4–inch thick, and 1 1/2 inches thick if you like your steak very rare. Be sure that you get this cut from your butcher, not the ends of the strip.

The steaks are to be fried very quickly; therefore they should be at room temperature before being put into the pan. In a heavy iron skillet placed over high heat add:
2 tablespoons sweet butter

Just before butter begins to burn, add to pan:
6 tenderloin steaks

When nicely browned on one side, turn and:
salt lightly with herb salt

Continue to cook until desired doneness.

In a separate skillet sauté until just done and soft to the touch:
6 large mushroom caps
2 tablespoons sweet butter

Lay sautéed mushrooms on each steak. Serve on hot plates with a bowl of Béarnaise sauce (*page 38*) on the side to spoon over them. What a delicious combination of flavors!

Serves 6

Tournedos Rossini

This is another famous way to serve the tenderloin filet.

Prepare tournedos and mushrooms as in previous recipe:
6 tenderloin steaks
6 mushroom caps

Fill each mushroom caps with:
**1/2–inch slice of paté de
    foie gras**

The paté (*page 49*) will not slice unless it is chilled. Roll it in waxed paper, chill and slice.

Serve with:
Béarnaise sauce (*page 38*)

Serves 6

Tournedos Zoia

Slice in 6 8-ounce slices:
3 pounds tenderloin filet

Braise until done but not too brown:
1/4 pound butter
3 cups onions, sliced thin

Add and continue to cook until just done:
**1 pound mushrooms,
   sliced thin**

Grind in mortar:
1/2 teaspoon meat herbs
1/2 teaspoon herb salt

Mix with:
**1 tablespoon beef
   concentrate** (*Bovril*)
Add to mushrooms and onions.

Mix together:
1/2 cup whole milk
1 cup Béchamel (*or rich cream*)
   sauce (*page 43*)
1 1/2 cups sour cream
1/2 teaspoon Kitchen Bouquet

Add to mushroom and onion mixture and stir in well. Reheat but do not cook as it tends to curdle.

Fry the beef filets lightly in a heavy iron pan, in sweet butter. Season with herb salt and serve on hot serving plates with the sauce spooned over each slice.

This is an excellent dish to serve if guests are late. The sauce keeps well heated, and the steaks can be cooked at the last moment, when the guests arrive.

Serves 6

Rye Steak

This recipe was given to me by Nancy Adams, our hostess for many years at the Ranch House.

Using a heavy iron skillet, sauté:
2 porterhouse steaks

Do not cook too much, as they will cook more in the sauce. Put the braised steaks aside on a platter, keeping them warm. In the skillet where the steaks were cooked, sauté gently until golden brown:
**4 green onions, white
   parts only, minced**

Add and mix in:
1 tablespoon beef extract

Italian Butter-Fried Beef

Now stir in and mix well:
1/2 cup rye whiskey
juice of 1/2 lemon

Simmer about 5 minutes, then taste. If it is too salty, thin with a little water but keep in mind that it must be rather salty to flavor the steaks. Put the steaks back in the pan and cook to your taste. Don't overcook them.

Serves 2

New York Steak Marinade

Combine the following ingredients and blend until smooth:
1/4 cup balsamic vinegar
2 teaspoons garlic, chopped
8 large sprigs rosemary

Now add and blend until just incorporated:
1/2 cup olive oil
1/2 cup walnut oil

Spread over New York steaks and refrigerate for 24 hours. Grill or barbecue.

One of the most interesting rotisseries I have seen was in Rome. In the wall at one end of the room was set an iron grate filled with red-hot coals. In front of it were the roasting pieces of beef on their turning rods sizzling appetizingly. This was the middle of summer and the weather was very hot. To protect the diners from the heat a wall of thick glass had been erected, and flowing down this wall was a steady stream of water, lowering the temperature as much by suggestion as by fact. The beef was served thinly sliced, with a wedge of lemon, and accompanied by a large green salad dressed with plenty of olive oil and vinegar — an excellent meal for a hot evening. You can serve your own version of this dish.

Have your butcher cut the tenderloin in very thin slices. Get out your old iron frying pan, place over high heat and add:
4 tablespoons sweet butter

Just before butter begins to burn, add to pan:
3 pounds thinly sliced tenderloin

Stir them around only enough just to cook them and add a sprinkling of herb salt. Serve them immediately, right from the skillet. Have handy a pepper mill and a plate of lemon wedges, the only seasoning necessary for this type of beef.

Serves 6

Gingered Top
Sirloin Steak

Don't skimp on the quality of the steak – nothing but the aged sirloin will do. Cook in your favorite way, over intensely hot coals or in buttered pan. Cook one side, turn, and immediately sprinkle on a mixture of finely chopped fresh ginger root, a little salt, and some freshly ground black pepper. Lightly press the seasoning into the meat with a spatula. The amount of fresh ginger used will depend on your liking for this seasoning. A squeeze of lemon may also be added.

Prime Rib with
Yorkshire Pudding

A reason for serving this fine cut of beef, besides its being traditional "Sunday food," is to have that delicious crusty pastry, Yorkshire pudding, as an accompaniment.

Does anyone have to be told how to cook this most popular roast? There are actually a number of ways to prepare it and perhaps you might like to try this one.

Have ready in whatever size you need:
prime rib roast

Rub the surface of the roast with:
herb salt
freshly ground black pepper

Roast in a 325° oven, allowing 20 minutes per pound (*15 minutes if you like the roast very rare*). When done, remove the roast and use the drippings in the Yorkshire pudding recipe which follows. If the roast is too rare for one of your guests, dip the slice in the hot juice for a minute or two, until it is the desired color. Skim and reserve fat and juice.

My English grandmother was a superb cook.

Yorkshire Pudding

*My maternal grandmother came from
Sheffield, England, and when I was young
she did much of the family cooking. I
remember especially her Sunday dinner of
roast beef and Yorkshire pudding. The roast
was well done so there would be plenty of
juice to make gravy. It was cooked in a
black iron pan about 10 by 14 inches,
which grandmother called a dripping pan.*

*When done the meat was removed from
the pan and kept warm. The "drippings"
were poured from the pan, then the fat
was skimmed and returned to it. Enough
pudding was made to fill the pan to about
an inch in depth. While the pudding was
baking, a rich brown gravy was made
by adding water to the juice and the right
amount of flour, salt and French capers.*

*The pudding was cut into squares,
loaded with gravy and served with slices of
beef and a vegetable, usually peas — and
we would enjoy a traditional English
Sunday dinner. The children tried to wangle
the corner pieces of the pudding because
they were so brown and crusty.*

*At the Ranch House we make
individual puddings, each one brown and
crusty, and fill them with the beef juice.
Here is how it is done.*

Prepare 4 medium–sized Pyrex
baking cups by brushing them with
fat from the roast. Put the greased
cups into the oven for at least
15 minutes with the oven quite
hot, 400°. While cups are heating,
mix in blender for 1/2 minute:
2 eggs
1 cup pie flour
1 cup milk
3/4 teaspoon salt

Take cups from oven and pour in
each a little fat (*not too much*). Fill
each cup about 3/4 full of batter and
return to a 400° oven. Bake until the
puddings rise up high and take on
a wonderful brown color. Usually
there is a hole in the center of each
baked pudding.

Mix in a little water and add to
beef juice:
1 beef extract cube

As you put each pudding on the
serving plate, fill the hole with
the beef juice mixture. (*If the baking
cup has been properly cured by the heating,
the pudding will lift out easily.*)

Serves 4

Beef Stroganoff

When we reopened the Ranch House and started serving meat, I had not eaten meat since my early youth and the flavors were almost forgotten. There I was, a reformed vegetarian, faced with learning how to prepare meat dishes. As a start, I decided I would achieve my own versions of three entrees, the names of which had attracted me: beef stroganoff, chicken cacciatore, and veal scaloppini. Boldly I chose the beef stroganoff first and called a friend in the Ojai Valley whose reputation as a cook was attested by all who have had the good fortune to enjoy her hospitality. She suggested recipes and I read others. Then I put them all aside and started to experiment.

Having read that the meat must be fried quickly and then sour cream added, I learned that part of the secret was to have the iron skillet very hot and to use suet instead of butter for the frying. Butter burns too easily, and the beef must be cooked rapidly, with great heat, or the meat juices will run out into the pan and the meat will be boiled instead of fried.

The day I started on the stroganoff, I had made Béchamel sauce, and it was cooling on the back of the stove. Since it had such a wonderful flavor, I added some of it along with the sour cream. Then I added fried mushrooms, a little tomato paste and other seasonings. The whole concoction was then heated in the double boiler. It is very important to let it mature for at least 1 hour, I have found, so that the flavors will blend completely.

Since I had never tasted beef stroganoff, I had only my own ideas to go on, and so could not imitate. As I concocted the dish for the next three or four times, I adjusted the proportions of the ingredients until I felt it was as good as I could make it.

Here is the recipe as we now serve it.

Slice into pieces about 1 1/2 inches long and 1/2 inch wide, and brown quickly in iron skillet greased with suet:

1 1/2 pounds beef, tenderloin
or tips

As meat is browned, put it in a double boiler to keep hot.

Sauté in butter:
4 ounces mushrooms, sliced
dash of herb salt

Mix well and add to mushrooms:
10 ounces sour cream
10 ounces Béchamel sauce
   (page 43)
1 tablespoon tomato paste
1/2 teaspoon salt
1/8 teaspoon black pepper,
   fresh ground

Add mixture to braised beef in double boiler and allow to mature for 1 hour. Then heat for 15 minutes and serve with rice.

Serves 4

Beef à la Mode

You can serve a large prime rib roast without wondering what you can do with the leftovers. Some people like this better than the prime rib dinner.

Cut into 1-inch squares, removing all fat:
1 pound cooked prime rib beef

Cook until smooth:
1 cup beef juice from pan
       drippings
2 tablespoons flour

Add and stir in well:
1 cup Béchamel sauce *(page 43)*
2 teaspoons beef concentrate
1/4 teaspoon Kitchen Bouquet
1/4 teaspoon lemon juice

When sauce is well blended add:
1 cup cooked small white
       onions, drained
1 cup cooked tiny carrots
       (optional)
the cubed beef

Reheat to serving temperature and allow to stand at this temperature for at least 30 minutes to blend flavors before serving. Serve in large casserole garnished with thin sliced mushrooms and a large dollop of sour cream. Accompany this dish with boiled potatoes or buttered noodles, wedges of tomatoes, and slices of green pepper.

Serves 6

*A few years ago
I was being taken
around Rome by
a friend.*

Beef Bali Hai

Many years ago in Paris a friend of mine took me to meet a man who had two restaurants, one for students located near the Sorbonne and very inexpensive, and another located on the Left Bank, for knowledgeable Frenchmen and lucky tourists like myself. The owner, Mr. So, was Chinese, born in Vietnam. One of his dishes was called Pork of the Five Perfumes, and I remember a soup made with shredded crabmeat, plenty of rice and Chinese parsley. The broth was chicken and the blend was perfect. When I came home I tried to duplicate some of his dishes. One of them I proposed to call Beef Vietnam, but the waitresses would not go along with that so we called it Beef Bali Hai.

Put into small frying pan that can be covered tightly:
2 tablespoons butter

Heat to browning point and then add and cover tightly:
**5 large green onions, cut
 diagonally
1/2 green pepper, cut into
 thin strips**

In about 10 seconds, no more, add, pouring around the edge of the lid so that it does not have to be lifted:
4 tablespoons hot water

Steam the vegetables for 1/2 minute only.

Mix together and heat, stirring until thickened:
**2 cups chicken broth
1 teaspoon cinnamon
3 tablespoons ginger syrup
2 teaspoons lemon juice
4 vegetable bouillon cubes,
 well dissolved in a
 little water
4 sprigs of wild anise,
 chopped fine
1 tablespoon cornstarch,
 dissolved in a little water**

Combine with steamed onions and green peppers, then add:
**2 pounds cooked prime
 rib beef, cubed
1/2 cup pignolia nuts**

Reheat and serve over turmeric rice.

Serves 8

Brandied Beef
(Beef Bourguignonne)

Cut into 1/2-inch cubes:
1/2 pound salt pork

Fry cubes in heavy iron pan until fat is cooked out and cubes are golden brown; then remove cubes and save them.

Cut into 1-inch cubes:
6 pounds round bone beef roast (*shoulder of beef*)

Brown beef cubes well on all sides in pork fat. Put pork and beef cubes in pressure cooker or heavy pot and add:
1/2 cup good brandy

Cover immediately while hot and refrigerate for 24 hours.

Add following ingredients to marinated beef and simmer, covered, in heavy pan until tender (*or at 15 pounds pressure for 12 minutes*):
1 cup water
2 tablespoons beef concentrate
      (*or 6 beef bouillon cubes*)
2 cloves garlic, minced
1/2 teaspoon meat herb blend
3 bay leaves
3/4 cup dry Burgundy
1/4 teaspoon fresh ground pepper

When done, drain juice and add to it enough water to make 3 cups. Thicken with:
4 tablespoons flour

Add to meat:
2 cups small whole cooked carrots
2 cups small whole cooked onions

Pour gravy over meat and vegetables. Reheat and let stand 30 minutes to blend flavors.

Serves 10

Fondue Bourguignonne

This famous Swiss fondue is served everywhere in Switzerland. It is not too difficult to prepare and can be one of the most festive dishes that can be imagined for a party.

You will need an alcohol stove and a metal pan to set over it, or the regular fondue casserole with its own heat; long wooden-handled forks with sharp tines to spear strips of beef, one for each guest; and for each guest a supply of wooden skewers.

Have your butcher cut into strips, 2 inches wide and 1/4-inch thick:
**beef tenderloin, 1/2 pound
   or more per person**

Slice the tenderloin strips into 1/2-inch wide pieces. Make sure it is at room temperature when ready to serve.

Put the following mixture in the fondue pot or pan so that the pot is about 2/3 full:
**1 part butter
2 parts peanut oil**

In the kitchen preheat the butter and oil until it is very hot and then place it over a high alcohol flame at the table to keep it hot. Place before each guest a dish of the tenderloin strips, ringed by little bowls of any of the following sauces. Each guest cooks his pieces of beef, one at a time in the hot oil, using the long-handled fork; then the cooked meat is taken off the fork with the skewer, dipped into any one of the sauces, and popped into the mouth.

How dare they serve meat.

Fondue Baccus

Sauces for Bourguignonne

Béarnaise: (*page 38*)

Russian: Mix together mayonnaise and catsup, to just the right flavor.

Mustard Mayonnaise: Mix dry mustard into mayonnaise.

Creamed Horseradish: Mix together sweet cream, dash of herb salt, 1 teaspoon lemon juice, good sharp horseradish.

Mushroom Sauce: Allow at least 1 large mushroom for each person. Mince mushrooms, add herb salt to taste, fry in butter until tender – a couple of minutes only – in a covered pan to preserve moisture. Sprinkle lightly with flour, stirring rapidly to prevent lumping, and cook to thick sauce consistency; mix in well a few drops of lemon juice.

Mayonnaise Oriental: Melt in a shallow pan, 2 tablespoons butter. Add 1 teaspoon curry powder, 1 minced green onion. Cook covered until onion is done. Stir this into 1 cup mayonnaise. Add and stir in: 1/2 teaspoon apricot jam, 1 teaspoon lemon juice. Mix well.

Green Onions: Chop very fine and sprinkle lightly with herb salt.

This is served like the Bourguignonne, except that the meat, cut in strips like the beef, is:
**veal tenderloin,
well pounded**

Cook in:
**white wine, heated and kept
very hot**

When heating the wine in the kitchen, put into it:
**1 onion, peeled and stuck
with 3 or 4 cloves**

Remove the onion when the wine is taken to the table.

Sauerbraten with Noodles

Combine in a stone crock:
1 pint vinegar
1/2 cup red wine
1 cup water

Add, being sure the liquid
covers it completely:
5 pounds beef chuck roast

Lay on, or push into the beef:
8 bay leaves
12 peppercorns
8 whole cloves

Marinate beef for 1 week in
refrigerator, turning every day so
that all sides of the meat will
be exposed to the marinade.
(Do not add salt or ground pepper at
this time, because salt will draw
out all the juices of the meat and make
it dry.) After 1 week, remove
and drain.

Put into heavy pot or pressure
cooker and heat very hot:
4 tablespoons fat

Sear beef well on all sides; then
spread over it:
2 cloves garlic, minced
7 turns of pepper mill
3 large carrots, sliced thin
3 large onions, cut coarse
4 tablespoons beef extract,
**   salted variety, or**
**   12 bouillon cubes**
2 cups marinade from crock
1 cup water

Cook, covered, very slowly for
several hours until beef is tender, or
for 12 minutes at 15 pounds in
pressure cooker *(cool and remove cap*
immediately, to prevent overcooking).
Thicken liquid with flour for gravy
and salt to taste. Serve with cooked
noodles and gravy.

Serves 8

Beef Italiano

Cut for broiling (*1/2 pound per portion*):
4 pounds top sirloin

Braise until just done:
**1 minced garlic clove in
2 tablespoons olive oil**

Add and cook until tender (*or for 2 minutes at 15 pounds in a pressure cooker*):
**1 onion, sliced thin
1/2 green pepper, sliced thin
6 sprigs oregano
2 sprigs fresh tarragon
6 sprigs basil
2 teaspoons bottled Italian
    sauce** (*optional*)

Slice medium thick:
4 cups fresh mushrooms

Toss lightly in:
2 tablespoons lemon juice

Drain mushrooms, retaining lemon juice, and sprinkle lightly with:
herb salt

Add mushrooms to vegetables and cook for 1 minute only in covered pan.

Mix together and cook until thickened; then add to vegetables:
**1 cup water
1 1/2 teaspoons beef concentrate
lemon juice from mushrooms
3 tablespoons flour mixed
    in a little of the water**

Broil the steak and then spread the vegetable mixture over it. Serve with lemon wedges to be squeezed over each portion.

Serves 8

Savory Meat Loaf

Mash together in a pan:
1/2 cup sunflower seeds
2 small onions, minced
2 eggs
2 tablespoons horseradish
1 teaspoon prepared mustard
1/2 green pepper, minced
1/4 cup tomato ketchup
1/2 teaspoon meat herb blend
1/8 teaspoon black pepper
1 1/2 teaspoons salt
1/4 pound sausage meat
1/2 cup stuffed olives
   (optional but very good)

Then add:
2 cups soft bread cubes
1/2 cup coffee cream

Add and mix well by squeezing
with the hands:
2 pounds ground chuck beef

Put into baking pan and press down
lightly, then pour over it:
1/4 cup rich chicken stock

Bake at 375° for about 1 hour, or
until done.

Serves 8 to 10

Lasagna

Prepare as directed on package:
lasagna noodles

Wash in cold water to remove
excess starch, then drain well.

Cook until soft:
3 cloves garlic, minced
2 onions, minced
4 tablespoons olive oil

Add and continue to cook gently
for 5 minutes:
1 green pepper, cut fine
1 cup mushrooms, sliced
2 bay leaves
2 teaspoons herb salt
1 teaspoon tomato herb blend

Add and cook for 1 minute:
2 6–ounce cans tomato paste
2 cups hot water
1 pound ground meat

Discard bay leaves. Put layer of
cooked noodles in a baking dish
which has been greased with:
olive oil

Spoon some of the sauce over the
noodles, then cover with:
Mozzarella cheese
Ricotta cheese *(or cottage cheese)*

Continue layering noodles, sauce and cheese. Bake at 350° for 30 to 45 minutes or until sauce begins to bubble at the edges and the cheese is melted. Serve with tossed green salad.

Serves 8

Swedish Meatballs

Mix well together:
**2 ounces pork sausage,
    seasoned by butcher**
3/4 cup onion, chopped fine
3 whole eggs
3/8 teaspoon nutmeg
**3/8 teaspoon fresh
    ground pepper**
**1/8 teaspoon powdered
    cardamom**
1/8 teaspoon savory herb blend
1/2 tablespoon salt
3 cloves garlic, minced fine

Toast and cut up fine:
2 slices white bread

Dissolve bread in:
3/8 cup coffee cream

Add this and the sausage and herb mixture to:
2 1/2 pounds ground beef

Mix well, squeezing with the hands; then form into small balls. Keep balls small so they will cook thoroughly. Fry them in oil or butter until lightly browned on all sides. Put meatballs in cooking kettle and add:
3/8 cup Burgundy
1/2 cup water
2 tablespoons chopped parsley

Cook 1/2 hour, then drain off juice into another pot and add to it:
3/4 cup sour cream
1/2 tablespoon beef extract
1/8 cup Burgundy
**1/2 cup water mixed with
    1 1/2 tablespoons flour**
1/4 teaspoon Kitchen Bouquet

Cook this sauce until thick and smooth, stirring well to avoid curdling sour cream. Pour onto the meatballs and simmer very gently for about 20 minutes. Do not boil.

Serves 6

Burgered Rice

Put in frying pan that can be tightly covered:

4 tablespoons butter or
**   margarine**
1 onion, sliced thin
1/2 green pepper, cut in
**   small cubes**
1/4 teaspoon herb salt

Cook until onion is clear, then add and brown:

1/2 pound hamburger

Add, then heat until very hot:

1/4 teaspoon marjoram
3 large sprigs parsley, minced
1/8 teaspoon black pepper
1/4 teaspoon garlic salt
1 pinch dill seeds
1/2 cup unwashed white rice

Mix and bring to boil:

1 cup water
1 1/2 teaspoons beef base

Add boiling water to burger mixture, cover and let simmer for 25 minutes.

Serves 4

Gypsy Beef with Noodles

Mix together and cook until partly clear but not done:

1 1/2 cups onions, minced fine
2 cloves garlic, minced
2 tablespoons fat

Remove to mixing bowl and add:

1 cup cooked rice
1/2 teaspoon dill seeds
3 1/2 teaspoons salt
1/2 teaspoon black pepper
1/4 teaspoon meat herb blend
1 pound seasoned sausage meat

Mix well and add:

3 eggs
5 pounds ground beef

Knead with hands until mixture is thoroughly blended.

Put into large kettle with tight cover:

10 unbroken outer leaves of
**   large cabbage heads**
1 cup water
2 tablespoons vinegar

Steam until leaves wilt and can be easily folded; then lay leaves on board. Divide meat mixture into 10 equal portions. Fold leaves around meat, wrapping securely, and tie across each way with string. Place in baking dish which can be tightly covered.

Cook for 5 minutes in covered pan:
1/2 cup water
5 stalks celery, sliced
3 large sprigs parsley, minced
1 tablespoon sugar
6 tablespoons vinegar
1/2 teaspoon salt
1/4 teaspoon black pepper

Remove from heat and stir in:
3 tablespoons tomato paste

Spoon sauce over cabbage rolls.
Bake at 350° for 1 hour or until done.

Top with sour cream and serve with
boiled noodles mixed with braised,
chopped green onions, chopped
parsley and plenty of butter.

Serves 10

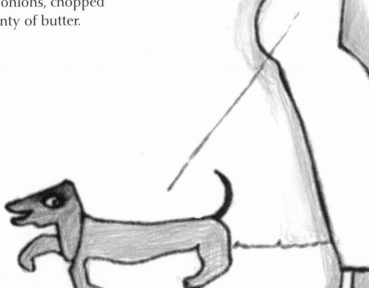

*I only dine
here because
of the scraps.*

Sunchoke Casserole

If you're wondering what "sunchoke" means, perhaps you will recognize Jerusalem artichoke as being the name of a native American tuber which was a staple of our Indians long before the white man came to trouble them. This root of the California sunflower is a valuable but not too well-known vegetable, low in starch but very high in protein, delicious in taste and of a wonderful texture, something like water chestnuts. They can be added raw to a mixed salad, sliced thin; served as a buttered cooked vegetable; and, as in this recipe, combined with other things. Where the name Jerusalem artichoke came from is still questioned, and now the vegetable people have decided to give them a new name — sunchokes.

Cook until clear:
1 clove garlic, minced
2 tablespoons butter
2 teaspoons herb salt

Wash well, being sure to get the dirt out of broken parts (*you do not need to peel*):
1 1/2 pounds sunchokes, sliced

Combine with:
1 onion, sliced thin

Add to cooked garlic with:
1/4 cup water

We hope you serve meat.

Cover. Cook until done, being careful not to overcook as they get mushy very quickly after they are done. They should be almost dry when finished, with no water to dilute the casserole; watch that they do not burn.

Braise:
1 pound ground chuck
1/2 teaspoon salt
2 tablespoons butter
1 bay leaf (*discard when cooked*)

Mix into the braised beef:
1/2 teaspoon marjoram
1/4 teaspoon thyme
a pinch of sage (*no more*)

Mix beef and vegetables together and put into a buttered casserole. Beat together and then pour over the casserole ingredients:
3 whole eggs
2 egg yolks
2 cups milk

Lay on top:
pimento strips

Bake at 350° until an inserted knife comes out clean, about 30 minutes. Here is a high protein dish that should please everyone, especially when served with corn on the cob.

Serves 6

Avocado Meat Loaf

Mix together well:
1 egg, well beaten
1 pound ground round steak
2 tablespoons onion,
    minced fine
2 tablespoons celery tops,
    chopped fine
4 tablespoons tomato ketchup
1 1/2 teaspoons salt
1 cup soft bread crumbs
1 avocado, peeled and
    cubed finely
2 tablespoons parsley,
    chopped

This amount will just fill a 12–hole muffin tin, well greased. Bake in very hot oven, 400°, for 20 minutes. Do not overcook, as an acid taste will develop from the avocado.

Gravy

Cook until clear:
1 tablespoon onion, minced
1 tablespoon butter

Brown in dry pan, stirring constantly:
4 tablespoons ordinary white
    flour (*do not allow it to get too*
    brown or to scorch)

Add and mix well, then cook until thickened:
cleared onions
1 cup water
1 beef or vegetable
    bouillon cube
1 tablespoon shredded
    Cheddar cheese
dash fresh ground pepper
1/2 teaspoon
    Worcestershire sauce
few drops lime or lemon juice

Add after gravy has thickened:
1/2 avocado, peeled and
    finely cubed

Gravy should be brown in color if the flour was done properly. A small amount of chopped parsley may be added if desired. Do not overheat after adding avocado, or an acid taste will develop.

Serves 6

LAMB

*Let's each choose
a different dish
and then share.*

*L*IKE VEAL, THE BEST LAMB IS THE YOUNGEST AND THEREFORE
NATURALLY TENDER. THIS IS WHAT IS MEANT BY SPRING LAMB. IF
IT ISN'T SPRING LAMB IT MUST BE HUNG — THAT IS, AGED — FOR TWO
OR THREE WEEKS TO TENDERIZE IT. YOU SHOULD MAKE SURE THAT
YOUR BUTCHER IS GIVING YOU AGED LAMB IF IT IS NOT SPRING
LAMB. OLDER LAMB THAT HAS BEEN PROPERLY AGED WILL BE QUITE
DELICIOUS, SO DO NOT HESITATE TO QUESTION YOUR BUTCHER, AND
DON'T BE PUT OFF WITH A FEW WORDS USED TO DELUDE YOU.

IN ENGLAND AND OTHER PARTS OF THE COMMONWEALTH,
MUTTON, THE OLDER ANIMAL, IS USED MUCH MORE FREQUENTLY
THAN IT IS IN THIS COUNTRY. IT IS HANDLED QUITE DIFFERENTLY

FROM LAMB; IT IS ALWAYS A BIT TOUGH AND SO MUST BE BOILED OR ROASTED A LONG TIME. IT IS IMPORTANT TO KNOW THAT BY COOKING YOU SIMPLY CANNOT MAKE TOUGH MEAT TENDER. YOU CAN COOK IT UNTIL IT FALLS APART BUT THE SHREDS WILL STILL BE TOUGH.

IN THIS COUNTRY, THERE IS AN OLD TRADITION OF SERVING MINT JELLY WITH ROAST LEG OF LAMB. AT THE RANCH HOUSE WE TRY TO AVOID THIS CLICHÉ BY SERVING CHUTNEY WITH THE LAMB, AND IT IS A HAPPY COMPANION TO THIS DISTINCTIVE MEAT. IN THE PAST, LAMB WAS ALWAYS ROASTED UNTIL IT WAS DULL GRAY. THIS TRADITION IS NOW DISAPPEARING. LAMB MAY BE ROASTED OR BROILED TO THE PINK STAGE, MUCH LIKE BEEF, IF ONE LIKES IT THAT WAY.

BECAUSE OF ITS STRONG FLAVOR, LAMB NEEDS A STRONG HERB OR SPICE TO GIVE IT THE PROPER ACCENT. AS A SEASONING FOR LAMB, BLACK PEPPER IS NOT NEARLY SO NECESSARY AS IT IS WITH BEEF, BUT LAMB SURELY MUST HAVE A HEARTY DOSE OF GARLIC. ONE OF THE BEST WAYS TO SEASON LAMB, ESPECIALLY IF YOU ARE MARINATING IT, IS TO GRIND UP THE HERBS TO BE USED WITH HERB SALT OR REGULAR SALT AND PLENTY OF FRESH GARLIC. THROUGH THE GARLIC, THE HERBS WILL PENETRATE THE MEAT. AN EXCELLENT HERB FOR LAMB IS THE PUNGENT ROSEMARY; ANOTHER IS SUMMER SAVORY. WINTER SAVORY CAN BE USED SPARINGLY – THOUGH I THINK IT TENDS TO IMPART THE DISTINCTIVE FLAVOR OF THE HOT DOG WHENEVER IT IS USED.

Stuffed Leg of Lamb

Have butcher bone, and save the bones:
6 pound leg of lamb

Put into mixing bowl:
2 cups cooked chicken, minced
    (*gizzards and hearts can be used*)
2 cups prepared stuffing bread

Mix together and heat:
**2 cups chicken broth, or 2
    chicken bouillon cubes
    and water** (*if cubes are used
    salt must be adjusted*)
1/4 teaspoon marjoram
1/4 teaspoon thyme
2 tablespoons orange juice
**3 tablespoons apricot jam or
    orange marmalade**
2 sprigs parsley, chopped
1/4 teaspoon black pepper
1 teaspoon salt (*less with cubes*)

Pour hot broth over stuffing.

Sprinkle boned lamb lightly with:
herb salt

Spoon stuffing into the lamb cavity.
Tie sides and ends together loosely
with string. Lay lamb on piece
of foil large enough so that the sides
will come up around but not fold

over the lamb when it is put in a
baking pan. Put extra stuffing around
lamb. Bake at 350º for 1 hour or
until done to taste. It will be juicier if
baked only until pink but it must be
cooked enough to be tender.

Stew for 30 minutes:
**lamb bones in
    2 cups water**

Take out bones and skim broth
well, then add to it:
any meat from bones
**1 tablespoon bottled
    Italian sauce**
**1 tablespoon beef extract or
    1 beef bouillon cube**

Adjust sauce with:
salt
dash black pepper

Thicken with:
**1 tablespoon flour,
    dissolved in water**

Serve lamb sliced with a mound of
stuffing topped with sauce. Chutney
is a good garnish for this dish.

Serves 10

Roast Prime Rib
of Lamb

Have your butcher cut in one
large piece, sawing the hinge part
just through for ease in carving:
8 ribs of young lamb

Mix in blender, as marinade:
1 cup olive oil
2 cloves garlic, minced
1/4 teaspoon powdered thyme
1/4 teaspoon powdered
   summer savory
1/2 teaspoon herb salt
1/2 teaspoon rosemary

Rub marinade on sides and
bottom of ribs and put them in
the refrigerator in a covered pan to
marinate for at least 24 hours; then
remove from refrigerator and let
stand until ribs reach room
temperature. Roast at 350° for
1 hour (*less, if you want it very pink*),
uncovered the last 15 minutes.
Cut 2 ribs for each serving.

Garnish with:
fresh mint or
   sprigs of rosemary

Serves 4

Rolled Leg
of Lamb

Make a pesto sauce in blender
with:
1 cup olive oil
1 cup basil
1 cup parsley
4 cups mint
1/4 cup garlic
1 teaspoon herb salt

Spread sauce inside boned lamb leg.
Rub outside with garlic oil and roast
for 1/2 hour at 500°.

Reduce heat to 375° and continue
to bake with:
1 cup port wine
3 carrots, cut coarse
3 stalks celery, cut coarse
2 sprigs of rosemary
2 bay leaves

When done remove fat from pan
gravy and add:
2 cups water
2 teaspoons beef extract

Simmer to reduce. Strain and
thicken with corn starch.

Serves 8

Lamb de Menthe

Braise in fat cut from the lamb until
it is brown:
**2 pounds leg of lamb, cut in
1-inch cubes**

Barely cover braised lamb with hot
water and cook until almost tender,
then add and cook until vegetables
are done but not mushy:
**1 large carrot, cut in
1/2-inch lengths**
**2 stalks celery, cut in
1-inch pieces**
1 green pepper, chopped coarse
1 teaspoon herb salt

Add and keep warm:
**2 teaspoons green crème
de menthe**
1 cup peas

Thicken juice with:
**1 tablespoon cornstarch,
mixed in a little water**

Serve with:
green or red rice

Serves 4

*That's the best
lamb I've tasted.*

Haricot des Mouton

One of the last restaurants to survive at Les Halles in Paris is Monteil's. It used to be the thing to do to go to the famed old market after the theater for a bowl of onion soup; people in full dress picked their way among the vegetable crates to find a place in the crowded restaurants along with shoppers, laborers and produce handlers. Jean Claude Boulet at Monteil's provided this recipe. It is still served in the daytime to the produce men. The market has been moved to Rungis, near the Orly airport; only remnants and memories linger at Les Halles.

Soak overnight, then cook in soaking water until tender:
1/2 pound navy beans
1 onion, stuck with 2 cloves
1 carrot, sliced thin
salt and pepper to taste

Remove onion and carrot from beans.

Braise:
3 pounds mutton, neck and breast, cut into chunks, in peanut oil

Mix together and flour lightly:
1 onion, chopped fine
1 carrot, chopped fine

Add to mutton and cook for 1 hour:
the floured, chopped vegetables
1 cup dry, white wine
1/2 cup water
1 tablespoon tomato paste
salt and pepper to taste
bouquet garni of:
   2 sprigs parsley
   1 sprig marjoram
   1 sprig thyme
   1 sprig basil

Combine mutton and bean mixtures. Discard herb bouquet. Serve accompanied by a large tossed salad.

Serves 6

Arabian Lamb & Lentils

The dusky flavors of lamb and lentils blend so well that I experimented until I developed a recipe that would incorporate both. Here is a most hearty dish.

Cut into 1-inch cubes:
3 pounds lamb shoulder
   (boned weight)

Braise lamb cubes until brown, using any type of oil, then combine with:
1/2 cup water
1 clove garlic, minced
1/2 teaspoon herb salt

Cook in a pressure cooker 12 minutes at 15 pounds or simmer in a heavy covered pan, adding more water if necessary, until the lamb is tender.

Combine in a pressure cooker or pan:
1 cup lentils
2 cups liquid, using lamb broth and water
2 celery stalks, chopped fine
1 onion, minced
2 garlic cloves, minced
1/2 teaspoon marjoram
1/4 teaspoon thyme
1/4 teaspoon rosemary

Cook at 15 pounds pressure for 14 minutes or simmer in a covered pan until the lentils are done.

Mix lamb and lentils together and keep warm over very low heat for at least 1/2 hour to combine flavors. Reheat and serve in small casseroles or shallow bowls.

Garnish with:
yogurt

The yogurt is essential and more than a garnish, because the tartness relieves the heavy flavor of the lamb and lentils.

Serves 8

Lamb Armenian

I cannot take credit for thinking of the entrée we call Lamb Armenian, but I do take credit for working out the final recipe. Jack Lynes from the Lamb Institute suggested it. While dining at the Ranch House, he asked if we ever served lamb. I said we didn't because I knew of no interesting way to prepare it. I didn't want to serve the usual leg of lamb available in most restaurants. He thought awhile and then said: "Why not stuff eggplant with lamb?"

This jarred my imagination and the next day I started experimenting. After trying various cuts, I chose leg of lamb for its texture, moisture and flavor when combined with the eggplant. Lamb shoulder will not do.

Here is the recipe as we now serve it.

Slice off the ends, about 3/4 inch, from the stem of:
6 average–size eggplants

Reserve ends. Hollow out the eggplant, leaving the sides about 3/4–inch thick. Be careful not to puncture the sides, or the juice will run into the pan. Steam the eggplant in a large, covered kettle for 9 minutes, using very little water. Do not overcook. Remove and cool immediately, draining out any juice.

Fry until it begins to lose its red color (*it is not supposed to be completely cooked*):
3 pounds leg of lamb, ground

Add to cooked ground lamb and mix together well:
3 tablespoons fresh mint leaves, minced
   (*more mint can be used*)
1/4 cup cooked rice
1/4 cup old–fashioned oatmeal
1 cup bottled Italian sauce
2 teaspoons herb salt
2 eggs

Stuff eggplants with this mixture. Put tops on eggplants and set them in a shallow pan. Bake at 400° uncovered for about 45 minutes.

Cook in pressure cooker for 30 minutes at 15 pounds or simmer in a kettle for several hours, adding more water as needed:
lamb bones
2 cups water

Skim off fat and remove bones.

Make sauce by heating in a
saucepan:

2 cups lamb broth
*(add more water, if necessary
to make 2 cups)*
2 teaspoons beef extract
(2 beef bouillon cubes)
**1 tablespoon bottled
Italian sauce**

Bring mixture to slow boil, then
slowly stir in a paste of:
flour and water

Continue to stir over heat until the
sauce is thickened, adding more
flour and water if necessary.

*Why not
stuff eggplant
with lamb?*

Cut stuffed eggplant into halves
and spoon sauce over
each serving.

Serves 12

Turla Quoi
(Lamb Ragout)

A guest at the restaurant one evening was a dark-eyed, dark-skinned beauty. She wrote out this recipe for me — one of her favorite dishes, she said. Serve with Turkish coffee.

Sauté:
**1 pound lamb, cubed and
    floured, in
    6 tablespoons olive oil**

Put lamb into casserole that can
be covered with:
**2 green peppers, quartered
3 large tomatoes, with
    seeds pressed out
2 cups string beans, cut
    across in half
1 small eggplant, peeled
    and cubed
2 carrots, cut in 1–inch pieces
1 large onion, cut into eighths**

Mix together and stir in gently:
**2 teaspoons salt
1 teaspoon black peppercorns
1 tablespoon paprika
1/4 teaspoon powdered cumin**

Add just enough water to be seen
through the top of the mixture.
Bake at 375° for about 2 hours,
covered. This dish can be served as
a casserole, or can be mixed with
lentils and served in small bowls.
While the lamb and vegetables are
baking, prepare lentils as follows:
**2 cups washed lentils
4 cups water
2 large onions, sliced thin
2 teaspoons salt
1/2 teaspoon powdered
    coriander
1 bay leaf** (*discard when cooked*)

Cook very slowly until lentils are
done; test after half an hour
(*or cook in pressure cooker for 15 minutes
at 15 pounds pressure*).

Serves 6

Pat Eaton's Moussaka

The wife of a long-time friend of mine, who had lived in Greece, gave me this wonderful recipe that her Greek cook used to make.

Stir into:
2 1/2 cups Béchamel
    sauce *(page 43)*
2 egg yolks

Brown in a frying pan:
2 pounds ground lamb
4 tablespoons olive oil

When brown, add and continue to cook for about 15 minutes:
1/4 teaspoon rosemary, chopped
3 large onions, minced
3 tablespoons tomato paste
1/2 cup red wine
3 tablespoons parsley, chopped
1/4 teaspoon cinnamon
1/4 teaspoon salt
1/4 teaspoon black pepper
4 ounces mushrooms, sliced

Cook the above until rather dry, then mix into the Béchamel sauce. Slice and broil until just done:
3 eggplants

Put a layer of the eggplant in a baking dish. Sprinkle with:
bread crumbs
1/2 cup Parmesan
    cheese, grated

Add a layer of the meat mixture, another layer of eggplant and so on, lightly topping the casserole with the grated cheese. Bake at 375° for about 1 hour or until brown on top. Cut into squares and serve.

Serves 8

Curried Lamb

Braise in oil until brown:
2 1/2 pounds lamb, cubed
  (leg of lamb is best)

Put browned lamb in pressure cooker with 1/2 cup water and cook for 10 minutes at 15 pounds pressure *(or add 1 cup water in a covered kettle and simmer until tender).*

Drain and reserve juice. *(Leftover cooked lamb and lamb gravy can be used instead of the above.)*

Cook until clear:
2 cloves garlic, minced
1 1/2 cups onions, minced
2 tablespoons butter

Add and cook slowly for at least 5 minutes on very low heat:
**2 1/2 tablespoons Madras
  curry powder**

Combine, then mix well into curry:
1 cup juice from cooked lamb
  (if necessary, add water to make 1 cup)
1/2 cup fresh coconut milk
2 tablespoons lemon juice
**3 tablespoons apricot or
  peach jam**
1 teaspoon salt

Thicken to a good consistency with:
**1 1/2 tablespoons cornstarch,
  mixed in a little water**

Steam in pressure cooker without cap or in covered kettle until just tender:
1 cup carrots, cut coarse
1 cup celery, cut coarse
1 cup onions, cut coarse

Salt to taste with:
herb salt

Then add to sauce.

Combine and gently mix together:
sauce and vegetable mixture
cooked lamb
1 cup uncooked peas, frozen

Keep warm for at least 30 minutes before serving to blend the flavors and thaw peas.

Serves 8

PORK

No dogs allowed.

Corn fed pork is not just a name or an advertising gimmick. This type of grain is required to put the right kind of fat on the animal and the right flavor in the meat. Iowa pork is probably the best in the country because the farmers raise so much good corn there. The meat itself should be white, like prime veal, with a tender texture. If you have had pork chops that you could never cook tender, probably they were not corn-fed pork. So you must find a butcher who is interested in getting the finest pork obtainable.

Pork is a sweet meat and it behaves well when a little brown or white sugar or syrup is added, as we use sweet sauces in baking hams. Therefore, herbs that have a sweetening effect go best with it, such as lemon verbena and pineapple sage; sweet marjoram and basil are also good in moderation, in combination with the first two and with some lovage added. Do not use strong herbs, such as rosemary or winter savory, or even most summer savory. These are too overpowering. The exception is sage used in sausage, but that is a completely different treatment and taste.

Pork Hawaiian

Place in stainless steel pan, fitting in tightly to cover bottom completely:

8 center–cut pork chops, cut 3/4–inch thick

Season chops lightly with salt, then spoon over them:

8 tablespoons candied ginger and syrup (*powdered ginger may be used, sprinkled lightly*)

Place on each chop:

1 leaf pineapple sage
1 leaf lemon verbena
fresh pineapple strips, sliced thin

Then sprinkle over each:

1 tablespoon brown sugar

Cover chops with:

fresh or canned pineapple juice mixed with 4 tablespoons vinegar
1/2 cup saki (*optional*)

Cover pan with waxed paper and bake at 400° for about 1 hour or until tender.

Pour off liquid and skim off fat, then thicken sauce with:

cornstarch, dissolved in a little water

Serve chops with thickened sauce spooned over them. Garnish with fresh coconut. Minted rice is a very good accompaniment to this dish.

Serves 8

Pork Tenderloin Munich

Cut into pieces that, when flattened with flat side of meat cleaver or large knife, will be about 2 inches in diameter:

1 pork tenderloin
(4 to 5 pounds)

Braise the slices in butter until done, very slowly at first, then with increasing heat *(they must not be pink in the center).*

To make sauce, sauté:
4 tablespoons butter
2 green onions, minced
(including tops)
1 clove garlic, minced
1/2 cup celery tops, minced

When done, stir in:
4 tablespoons flour

Add, cook and stir until thick:
2 cups chicken broth
1 teaspoon basil
2 dashes nutmeg
2 teaspoons beef extract
(2 beef bouillon cubes)
1/4 cup dry sauterne

When thickened, add:
1/2 cup coffee cream
1/2 cup sour cream

To serve, spoon sauce over tenderloin pieces. A light sprinkling of Parmesan cheese may also be added if desired. Crisp shoestring potatoes are an admirable companion to this dish, or potato pancakes can be the accompanying starch. Another suggestion is homemade boiled noodles tossed with fried bread crumbs and a bit of onion salt.

Serves 8

Pork Chops
with Pineapple

Fry in heavy iron skillet:
**pork chops, with the
 tenderloin left in
pineapple rings**

Sprinkle each side as they
cook with:
herb salt

The juices of the pork should
give the pineapple a nice brown
color. Serve with steamed rice
and pour the pan juices over it.

Pork with Brandied
Plum Sauce

Sauté:
**2 tablespoons butter
1 teaspoon minced garlic
1 teaspoon minced ginger
1 cup celery, chopped
1 cup onions, chopped**

Add to the above and bring to
a boil:
**1/2 cup plum purée
1 teaspoon minced lemon
 verbena
1 teaspoon pineapple sage
1/8 teaspoon black pepper
1 teaspoon herb salt
2 tablespoons white sugar
2 tablespoons cornstarch,
 mixed with water
2 tablespoons soy sauce**

When thick, add and stir in:
1/8 cup Bouchant liqueur
 (orange flavor)

Slice roasted pork loin or
tenderloin very thin and spoon
over it the above sauce.

Garnish with:
herb leaves

Serves 6

Pork Cointreau

So you want a special roast for a special dinner? Well, here it is.

Have the butcher bone:
**2 pork loins, leaving in
    tenderloin**

Then have him cut a strip of the best:
sirloin of beef

This strip should be the same length as the pork loin and about 1 inch thick and 2 inches wide. Have him tie the 2 loins together with the beef inside, making a long rolled roast. The ties should be about 1 inch apart all along the roast.

When you are ready to start cooking the roast, stand it on end and with the handle of a wooden spoon make 4 openings between the segments of the roast.

Now mix together:
2/3 cups soy sauce
about 1/3 cup Cointreau
    (orange liqueur)
1/2 teaspoon herb salt

Spoon some of the Cointreau sauce into each of the openings in the roast, reserving a few spoonfuls to brush on the top and for basting. Bake at 350° for about 1 1/4 hours,
basting every 15 minutes with the extra sauce and the pan juices. The beef should be pink when done.

Liquefy in blender:
1 28–ounce can fruit cocktail
3 tablespoons Cointreau
1/4 teaspoon herb salt
2 drops green coloring
9 drops red coloring

Bring mixture to boil in saucepan and thicken with:
**1 tablespoon cornstarch,
    dissolved in a little water**

The sauce should be just runny enough to be attractive when spooned over the slices of meat. Keep the parts of the roast together when slicing, for eye appeal.

Broil in:
butter
slices of pineapple
    (1 for each serving)

Fill holes in pineapple with:
chopped walnuts

For each serving, spear on a toothpick:
1 piece spiced cantaloupe
1 green cherry
1 red cherry

Gingered Ham
& Oranges

Stick the toothpicks in the sliced
pineapple, red cherry on top,
and with a spatula put a pineapple
slice on each serving of meat; or
serve the roast on a heated platter,
garnished with pineapple slices.
Between the pineapple
slices sprinkle:
**coconut curls, heated
    and lightly salted**

*All this makes a very dramatic entrée which
will bring exclamations from your guests,
and none of it is a bit difficult to do!*

Serves 8 to 10

*A special roast
for a special dinner.*

Place in shallow baking pan:
**1 center–cut slice of ham,
    1–inch thick**

Spread over ham:
**candied ginger and syrup,
    to taste** (*not too much*)
**pickled onions, chopped
8 1/4–inch thick slices fresh
    orange, with skin on**

Spoon on each orange slice:
1 teaspoon orange marmalade

Bake at 400°, uncovered, for about
45 minutes (*longer will tend to dry it
out*). When done, remove ham and
thicken sauce in pan with:
**cornstarch, dissolved
    in a little water**

Spoon sauce over ham and garnish
with the baked orange slices.

Serves 6 to 8

Pork Polynesian

Have butcher cut:
**6 pork chops, 1 1/2-inches
thick, with tenderloin left in**

Ask the butcher to cut a pocket in
each chop, starting at the small
end, but without cutting through,
so that the stuffing will not leak.

Braise chops on each side in fat
after sprinkling them with:
herb salt

Cook until clear and done:
**1 small onion, chopped fine
1 clove garlic, minced
2 tablespoons butter**

Add and continue to cook
until smooth:
3/4 teaspoon curry powder

Mix together and add:
**1 28-ounce can fruit cocktail
and juice
1 1/2 teaspoons lemon juice**

Add, cook and stir until thick:
**2 teaspoons cornstarch ,
dissolved in very little water**

Using only the fruit, stuff each pork
chop and close the end with a
toothpick. Lay chops in baking pan
and pour over them the remaining
juice mixed with:
1/4 cup pineapple juice

Sprinkle lightly with:
herb salt

Cover pan with waxed paper (*don't
use foil as it will steam them instead of
baking them*). Bake at 350° for about
1 hour.

Drain off juice and thicken it
slightly with:
**1 teaspoon cornstarch,
mixed in a little water**

For color, add:
red coloring (*1 or 2 drops only*)

Serve sauce over chops,
garnished with:
**slices of fresh papaya
freshly grated coconut
macadamia nuts, chopped**
(*optional, for glamour and texture*)

Serves 6

Baked Ham with Curried Fruit

Have butcher draw the bone from:
1 ham (*this makes it easier to slice*)

Bake ham according to directions on package or from butcher. The last hour of baking, baste the ham with the following sauce.

Drain, reserving syrup:
1 16–ounce can each of peach, pear and apricot halves

Combine 4 cups of the fruit syrup with:
3/4 cup water
3 tablespoons lemon juice
2 tablespoons brown sugar
2 teaspoons curry powder
2 tablespoons cornstarch, dissolved in a little water

Cook and stir over low heat until the sauce is thick.

Place the drained fruit in a baking pan, pit side up, and spoon on each piece of fruit the following mixture which has been heated until dissolved:
4 tablespoons butter, melted
1/2 cup brown sugar
2 tablespoons curry powder

Bake fruit for 15 minutes at 325°. Serve with ham slices. Rice with a dash of turmeric makes an excellent accompaniment.

Serves 8

Pork Chops Iowa Style

Braise on both sides in fat:
**4 large, thick loin chops with
tenderloin left in**

Salt on both sides with:
herb salt

Lay braised chops in a casserole
that can be tightly covered.

Mix together and spread over chops:
**1 28-ounce can cream-style
corn with liquid
1/2 green pepper, chopped
very fine
1 pimento, chopped fine
2 tablespoons coffee cream
mixed with
1 tablespoon flour
1/2 teaspoon meat herb blend
1/2 teaspoon herb salt**

Cover tightly and bake at 350° for
about 1 hour.

Remove chops and adjust thickness
of sauce by thinning with cream,
if too thick, or adding flour
and water paste over heat, if
too thin. Serve sauce over chops.
Mashed potatoes are almost a must
with this Midwestern dish, which
was so much enjoyed by my family
on cold wintry nights.

Serves 4

VEAL & VENISON

*I'm going to
the Ranch House
for dinner.*

$\mathcal{S}$EVERAL OF THESE VEAL RECIPES COME FROM
EUROPE WHERE I LEARNED TO PREPARE THEM WITH TRUE
VEAL, WHICH IS THE MEAT OF THE YOUNG CALF THAT HAS
NEVER FED ON ANYTHING BUT ITS MOTHER'S MILK. THE
MEAT IS WHITE AND VERY TENDER AND OF A DELICATE
AND DISTINCTIVE FLAVOR. IT NEEDS BARELY ANY COOKING
AND MANY PEOPLE LIKE TO EAT IT ACCOMPANIED ONLY BY A
WEDGE OF LEMON TO SQUEEZE OVER IT. IN THE DAIRY

COUNTRIES SUCH AS DENMARK AND HOLLAND, THERE IS AN AMPLE SUPPLY OF THESE SMALL YOUNG ANIMALS, AND WHITE VEAL IS PLENTIFUL EVERYWHERE IN EUROPE.

WHITE VEAL IS RARE IN THIS COUNTRY, ESPECIALLY IN THE WESTERN STATES. IT IS LESS PROFITABLE TO SLAUGHTER ANIMALS WEIGHING UNDER 400 POUNDS; THIS MEANS THAT THE CALVES HAVE STARTED TO FEED AWAY FROM THEIR MOTHERS. THE MEAT, THEREFORE, BEGINS TO TURN RED AND THE TEXTURE CHANGES FROM VERY SOFT TO FIRM. ALTHOUGH WE SPEAK OF THIS AS VEAL, IT IS REALLY ONLY YOUNG BEEF WHICH HAS ALREADY BEGUN TO TAKE ON THE CHARACTERISTIC BEEF FLAVOR. IF YOU CANNOT FIND THE WHITE VEAL, YOU WILL NEED TO COOK THE MEAT A LITTLE LONGER THAN THE TIME GIVEN. WHEN YOU CAN GET WHITE VEAL, GIVE IT THE GENTLEST TREATMENT, AND ENJOY A SPECIAL TREAT.

THE HERBS TO USE WITH VEAL SHOULD BE THE DELICATE ONES LIKE SWEET MARJORAM, BASIL, AND A LITTLE PINCH OF THYME, PLUS PARSLEY. THE ADDITION OF CHOPPED LOVAGE IS ACCEPTABLE. NEVER USE A STRONG HERB, ESPE-CIALLY WITH WHITE VEAL — IT WILL KILL THE FLAVOR. VEAL COOKED IN WINE IS AN EXTRAORDINARY COMBI-NATION. IMAGINE TENDER MORSELS POUNDED THIN AND GENTLY SIMMERED IN A FINE WHITE RHINE WINE.

Veal Allegro

Slice in thin slices:
**1 very young and tender
veal tip** (4 to 5 pounds)

Braise in:
butter

Season to taste with:
herb salt

Place slices on hot platter
and spoon over them the
following sauce.

Braise:
**2 green onions, sliced,
in 4 tablespoons butter**

Stir in:
4 tablespoons flour

Add and stir until thickened:
**1 pint coffee cream
2 teaspoons beef extract**
(2 beef bouillon cubes)

When thick, add:
**8 ounces mushrooms and
stems, sliced
2 apples, peeled, quartered,
cored and sliced, following
the curve of the apples**
(making nearly flat pieces)

Pound together in mortar and add:
**1/2 teaspoon herb salt
pinch each of basil, marjoram,
thyme, celery seed
1/2 teaspoon minced parsley**

Then add:
**4 tablespoons sherry
1/2 teaspoon lemon juice**

Simmer this sauce until apples
just begin to get tender.
Mushrooms and apple slices
should not be overcooked, but
cooked just until the raw taste
and texture have disappeared.
This is the most important part
of the entire preparation.

Serves 8

Veal François

Cut into 1-inch cubes and braise
until well browned:
6 pounds veal (*older veal
can be used for this recipe*)
1/4 pound butter

Put veal cubes into saucepan,
leaving butter in frying pan.

Add to veal cubes and cook
until just tender:
1/2 cup sherry
1/2 cup water
2 tablespoons chicken base
1/2 bay leaf (*discard when cooked*)

Add to butter in frying pan:
1 pound mushrooms, sliced
1/2 teaspoon herb salt
1 pint coffee cream
**3 tablespoons flour, mixed
in a little of the cream**

When veal is tender, add it to
the mushroom mixture and adjust
seasoning with:
salt
good dash black pepper

Heat to serving temperature and
serve with rice.

Serves 8

Veal Hungarian

*This is a very good dish for entertaining
as it will not be spoiled if guests are
late. Older veal can be used, but must be
cooked longer.*

Cut in 1-inch cubes and braise:
6 pounds veal shoulder
(*boned weight*)
1/4 pound butter

Add and cook 6 minutes:
1 cup water
4 cups onions, sliced
2 cups carrots, sliced
2 cups celery, sliced thin
4 cloves garlic, minced
4 bay leaves (*discard when cooked*)
4 tablespoons paprika
2 cups chicken stock
4 tablespoons chicken base

Add and cook very slowly until
veal is almost tender:
4 tablespoons tomato paste
**4 tablespoons flour, mixed
with a little water**

Veal Minnesota

Have butcher cut 1/2-inch thick strips into 2-inch pieces:
3 pounds veal tip

Pound veal into scallops and braise in:
4 tablespoons butter

Remove veal from frying pan and lay it in a shallow baking pan. Braise in the butter from the veal:
1/2 cup mushrooms, sliced

Add to mushrooms:
1/2 cup sherry
2 cups chicken stock
1/2 teaspoon herb salt

Grind in mortar and add to mushroom mixture:
1/2 teaspoon salt
1 large sprig basil
2 sprigs lemon thyme
1 large sprig lemon balm
2 leaves costmary
3 sprigs marjoram
1/2 teaspoon celery seeds

Wash and add to mixture:
1/2 cup wild rice

Pour mixture over veal, cover and bake for 1 hour at 400°. Serve in individual casseroles.

Serves 6

Add and cook until veal is completely tender:
2 cups green peppers, sliced
2 cups sliced sweet red peppers
  (*if available*), **or**
  1 3-ounce can pimentos, chopped

Serve in individual casseroles over:
peasant noodles

Garnish with:
dollop of sour cream
parsley, chopped

Serves 12 or more

Veal Scaloppini

Here is the third of those remembered names that became one of our menu standards when we started serving meat at the Ranch House. As with the other two, I first read recipes, then put them aside, and through experimentation and refinement arrived at this recipe.

Have butcher slice into strips,
1 1/2 by 3 inches, 1/4–inch thick:
1 veal tip *(4 or more pounds)*

Dip slices lightly in:
Parmesan cheese, grated

Brown quickly in butter in very hot skillet. Keep pan scraped and save scrapings.

Set browned veal aside and sauté in pan where it was browned, adding scrapings:
1 1/2 cups sliced mushrooms
4 tablespoons butter

Add and bring to boil:
1 cup sherry
1/2 cup Sauterne
1/2 cup Chablis
1/2 cup Béchamel sauce
   (page 43)
1 teaspoon beef extract
   (1 beef bouillon cube)
1 1/2 teaspoons herb salt
1/2 teaspoon savory
   herb blend
1/2 cup water
dash cayenne or
   black pepper

Mix well in skillet and cook until well blended.

Lay the strips of veal in a baking pan and pour the sauce from the skillet over them. Bake tightly covered until tender, about 45 minutes to 1 hour, at 400°. Remove veal and thicken gravy with a little flour mixed in water. Serve in small casseroles.

Serves 8

Veal Parisian

Cut into strips 2 inches by 1/2 inch:
1 veal tip (*4 to 5 pounds*)

Pound strips into scallops; then
sear quickly in butter in heavy iron
skillet, keeping pan very hot so
meat will not lose juice. Remove
meat and pour into skillet:
sherry to a depth of 1/2 inch
1 1/4 cups sour cream, beaten
   to take out lumps

Scrape up fryings in skillet and stir
mixture until smooth, then add:
2 tablespoons beef extract
1 cup water
fresh–ground black pepper
1 bay leaf (*discard when cooked*)

Bring mixture to boil, then pour
over veal scallops in baking
dish. Cover tightly and bake for
1 1/2 hours or until done.

To make sauce, wash and drain:
4 ounces French sorrel, tops only

Cook tops 2 minutes in pan with:
2 tablespoons water

Put through sieve and add:
1 1/2 cups sour cream
1/2 teaspoon herb salt
1 or 2 drops green coloring

Thicken sauce by cooking slightly,
then pour over baked scallops in
casserole and serve.

Serves 8

*What does he put
in the champagne
cocktails?*

Preparation of Sweetbreads

Wash the sweetbreads and squeeze all dark places free of blood; then soak them in cold water for at least 1 hour. Blanch the sweetbreads by boiling in water for 20 minutes. Drain them, and plunge them into cold water; then soak them another 30 minutes. Separate them into 1 1/2-inch pieces, removing any membranes and dark parts.

Sweetbreads Alsace

Sauté for about 10 minutes or until tender:
**3 pounds prepared
    sweetbreads in
    6 tablespoons butter**

At the last minute or two add:
**12 medium–sized
    mushrooms, sliced**

Mix together:
**1/2 cup sherry
3 teaspoons beef extract
1 teaspoon herb salt
1/4 teaspoon white pepper
1 cup whipping cream**

Mix together:
**3 tablespoons flour
3 tablespoons butter**

Add to sherry mixture, heat and stir until it thickens; then add and stir until smooth:
**6 tablespoons sherry
6 tablespoons coffee cream**

Mix sweetbreads and sauce together and serve in individual casseroles on:
thin slices of buttered toast

Serves 6

Sweetbreads au Crème

Prepare as directed (*page 248*), then sauté for 10 minutes:
2 pounds sweetbreads in 6 tablespoons butter

At the last minute or two add:
1/2 pound large mushrooms, sliced

Heat to boiling point:
1 pint coffee cream
1/2 pint whipping cream
1 bay leaf (*discard when cooked*)

Combine and stir into cream:
2 tablespoons butter
4 tablespoons flour

Add:
2 teaspoons beef extract

Pound in mortar and add:
1/2 teaspoon herb salt
1 sprig marjoram
1 sprig basil
1/8 teaspoon white pepper

Cook and stir sauce until thick over low heat; then stir in well:
2 ounces sherry (*or brandy*)

Mix sauce with sweetbreads and serve with:
cooked rice

Garnish with:
parsley, minced
paprika

Serves 6

Broiled Sweetbreads

Prepare as previously directed
(*page 248*):
2 pounds sweetbreads

Broil them until nicely done and
tender, about 10 minutes, not
too near the grill to burn them.
Set aside and keep warm.

To make the sauce, cook
until tender:
2 shallots, chopped
2 sprigs marjoram, chopped
2 sprigs basil, chopped, in
    1/2 pound butter

When just done, add and mix well:
1/2 cup parsley, minced fine

Put cooked sweetbreads on hot
platter and pour the sauce over
them. It should be slightly brown.

Garnish with:
6 tablespoons bread crumbs,
    lightly browned in
    4 tablespoons butter

Serves 6

Venison Grenadier

In a saucepan combine the
following ingredients and simmer
until reduced by half:
1/2 cup pomegranate juice
1/2 cup beef stock
1/4 cup Madeira wine
1/4 cup brandy
1 clove garlic, crushed
1 sprig thyme
2 tablespoons pineapple juice
5 juniper berries, crushed
4 turns pepper grinder
1/2 teaspoon beef extract

When reduced, strain and thicken
slightly with corn starch. Serve over
thinly sliced venison medallions
which have been quickly sautéed.

Serves 6

DESSERTS

We want Fig Pie!

$\mathcal{T}$HERE IS GOOD REASON FOR MY INTEREST IN FOOD: AN AWARENESS OF THE OPPORTUNITIES FOR CREATING AN ATMOSPHERE OF GENTLE GOODWILL, AND A KIND OF THANKFULNESS FOR THE BLESSINGS OF GOOD FOOD AND COMPANIONSHIP ENHANCED MY MEMORIES OF OUR FAMILY LIFE WHEN I WAS YOUNG.

WE SEEMED ALWAYS TO HAVE FAMILY FRIENDS AT OUR TABLE, ESPECIALLY FOR SUNDAY DINNER, AND THOSE WHO LIVED ALONE WERE THE ONES MOST FREQUENTLY SOUGHT OUT TO SHARE OUR TABLE JOY. DAD WAS THE MEAT COOK FOR THESE OCCASIONS, AND OF COURSE MOTHER DID THE PASTRIES. I HAD A HAND IN THE SALADS AND VEGETABLES,

AND MY SISTER DOROTHY TOOK CARE OF THE DINING ROOM ARRANGEMENTS.

MY BROTHER DONALD'S MAIN FUNCTION IN THESE COMBINED FAMILY EFFORTS SEEMED TO BE THAT OF EATING, AND THIS HE DID AT MEALTIMES, AND ANY OTHER TIME, WITH GREAT APPRECIATION. HOWEVER, I MUST TELL YOU THAT HE WAS A COOKIE BREAKER. MOTHER KEPT A COOKIE JAR FILLED, AND IT WAS HIS HABIT TO REACH IN OFTEN AND BREAK OFF HALF A COOKIE. AS A RESULT — I THINK HE MUST HAVE FELT THAT HE WAS USING RESTRAINT IN TAKING ONLY HALF A COOKIE — WE OFTEN HAD, AT THE BOTTOM OF THE JAR, MANY TIRED LITTLE PIECES THAT HAD FILTERED DOWN.

COOKBOOKS HAVE SO MANY WONDERFUL DESSERTS, ONE WOULD THINK THERE COULD BE NO NEED FOR MORE. STILL, WE INCLUDE SOME THINGS THAT WE THINK MIGHT TITILLATE YOUR PALATE. THEY ARE MY OWN CREATIONS, AND MOSTLY THEY CAME OUT OF NECESSITY. SOMEONE REMARKED ABOUT SOMETHING; SOMEONE ASKED FOR SOMETHING WHICH WE DID NOT HAVE — AND I HAVE TRIED TO INVENT THINGS I FELT PEOPLE WOULD LIKE. YOU SEE, WE HAVE CUSTOMERS WHO COME HERE SO OFTEN THAT THEY HAVE BECOME VERY GOOD FRIENDS, AND I LOVE NOTHING BETTER THAN TO TRY AND FIND NEW THINGS TO DELIGHT THEM.

Frosted Creams

Mix together:
1 cup white sugar
1/2 cup butter or
      margarine, melted

Add and mix:
1 cup molasses
2 eggs, beaten
1 cup buttermilk or
      sour milk

Mix well together:
1 teaspoon cinnamon
1 teaspoon ginger
1 teaspoon salt

Add and mix:
3 cups flour
1 1/4 teaspoons baking soda

Combine all ingredients.

Grease two 10 by 15-inch pans and divide the batter between them, spreading it evenly so that it will bake properly. Bake at 450° for 15 minutes on the lower shelf of the oven, then put on top shelf for about 10 minutes more or until the batter slightly leaves the sides of the pan. Remove and ice immediately.

The icing is made by mixing together powdered sugar and a little milk. Some of the brown top of the cake will show through the icing, and perhaps this is where the cookies get their name. This icing should be thin, and put on sparingly so that it will not overpower the flavor of the gingerbread (*for that is really what it is*).

It should be cut immediately into squares, and when cool enough should be moved from the pan to prevent sweating. The cookies should be very thin, and cut 24 squares to each pan. Children love them for their wonderful molasses flavor pepped up with spice.

Drop Cookies

*As the name implies, drop cookies should
be dropped from a spoon and then spread
evenly with a rubber spatula so they will
rise evenly. If this is not done they rise
up in the center more like small cakes, and
the right texture is lost.*

*It is also important, when you are
going to use the cookie sheets or pans a
second time in your cookie-baking session,
that they have time to cool off before the
second batch of cookies is dropped on them.
If they are the least bit warm, the cookies
tend to melt before they go into the oven,
and this will destroy the texture.*

Oatmeal Sesame Cookies

Mix together:
1/2 cup oil
**1 1/2 cups dark–brown
     sugar**
1 egg, well beaten

Combine and mix in:
**2 tablespoons milk or
     buttermilk**
1 1/4 cups rolled oats
1/2 cup raisins
3/4 cup sesame seeds
     (or sliced hazelnuts)

Sift together and mix in:
**1 1/4 cups whole–wheat
     pastry flour**
1/2 teaspoon baking soda
1/4 teaspoon salt
1/2 teaspoon nutmeg
1 teaspoon cinnamon

Drop from spoon dipped in cold
water. Bake at 375° until brown.

Makes about 36 cookies

Sugar Drop Cookies

Cream together:
2 cups sugar
1/2 pound butter
   (at room temperature)

Add and mix well together:
2 eggs, beaten lightly

Then stir in:
1 cup sour milk or
   buttermilk

Combine and mix in:
4 cups flour
1 teaspoon baking soda
1 teaspoon salt
1 teaspoon baking powder
1 teaspoon nutmeg
1/2 teaspoon vanilla
1 teaspoon caraway seeds
   (optional)

Drop from spoon on baking sheets, spread with spatula and bake at 350° until nicely brown. Remove from sheet immediately and cool on wax paper.

Makes about 48 cookies

Applesauce Cookies

Cream together:
1/2 pound butter
   (at room temperature)
2 cups sugar

Add and beat in well:
1 egg

Mix together and beat in:
3 cups flour
1 teaspoon cinnamon
1/2 teaspoon powdered cloves
1/8 teaspoon salt
1 teaspoon baking soda

Add and stir in well:
1 cup unsweetened,
   thick applesauce
1 cup chopped walnuts

Drop on greased cookie sheet, spread with spatula and bake at 425° until brown.

Makes about 36 cookies

Sour Cream Cookies

Cream together:
1/2 pound butter
   (at room temperature)
2 cups white sugar

Add and beat in well:
2 eggs

Then add and beat in:
1/2 pint sour cream
1 teaspoon baking soda
1 teaspoon vanilla
1/2 teaspoon powdered
   cardamom seed *(optional)*
1/2 teaspoon salt

When soft ingredients are well
mixed, stir in:
4 cups sifted flour

Spoon onto greased cookie
sheet and spread with spatula.
Bake at 425° for about 10 minutes.
Remove from sheet to cool.

Makes about 36 cookies

Molasses Cookies

*The thought of these old-fashioned cookies,
served hot with a glass of cold rich milk,
wafts me back to a Midwestern farmhouse
kitchen where hungry boys home from
school made them disappear like magic.*

Beat well together:
1 cup sugar
1/2 cup molasses
1/4 pound butter
   (at room temperature)

Add and beat in:
2 eggs

Then add and beat in:
1/2 cup sour milk or buttermilk
2 teaspoons baking soda

Add and mix in gently:
3 cups sifted flour
1/2 teaspoon baking powder
1 teaspoon salt
1 teaspoon cinnamon
1 teaspoon powdered ginger
1/4 teaspoon powdered cloves
1/2 cup raisins *(optional)*

Drip from spoon onto greased
cookie sheet, spreading around with
a spatula. Bake at 425° until done,
perhaps 10 minutes. Remove
immediately from sheet to cool.

Makes about 36 cookies

Bananas Flambé

Mix together over low heat:
1/2 cup fresh orange juice
rind of 1 orange, grated
1/2 cup water
2 tablespoons Benedictine
2 tablespoons Curaçao
1 cup dark–brown sugar
1/4 teaspoon ground
  coriander seed
1/4 teaspoon fresh
  ground nutmeg

Heat this mixture only enough to dissolve the brown sugar.

Mix together:
1 teaspoon cream of tartar
4 cups water

Peel:
6 large firm bananas
  (*without brown spots*)

Dip peeled bananas into cream of tartar solution to keep them from turning dark. Drain them and then cut across and lengthwise to make 4 equal pieces of each banana.

Melt in a large frying pan, preferably copper clad:
4 tablespoons butter

Lay half of the banana pieces in skillet, cut side down. Fry until lightly brown, shaking skillet so they do not stick. Turn over and fry a little longer, but not until brown or they will fall apart; keep them whole. Before frying the rest of the bananas, melt in the skillet:
4 tablespoons more butter

When all bananas are fried, put them in a chafing dish or other dish that can be kept hot. Pour the hot orange mixture over them. You are now ready to flame the bananas. Warm gently over very low heat (*do not overheat or the alcohol will evaporate*):
1/2 cup brandy
  (*flaming type preferably, with high percentage alcohol*)

Pour warm brandy into small serving vessel that can be kept hot and place it and the chafing dish of bananas on the table. Turn off the lights – candlelight only for this. Light the brandy and immediately pour it over the bananas. If the banana mixture has been kept hot, the brandy will continue to burn as you serve each guest a flaming portion. All this is really not difficult to do, and is dramatic and extra delicious also. Just follow directions exactly as given, especially regarding temperatures.

Serves 6

Old-Fashioned
Boston Cream Pie

Many years ago I ran a wholesale pie bakery in Columbus, Ohio, and of course developed and collected many, many pie recipes. Over the years some of these recipes were misplaced, among them this recipe. Without it I could not recreate the rich, delicious cake (for it really is a cake) that I remembered. Recently, I found the recipe. Here it is, one of those priceless, simple-but-wonderful recipes that good cooks love. Its uniqueness is the way in which the custard filling is made and how the eggs and sugar are combined.

Beat at high speed for 15 minutes
(this is very important):
1 cup whole eggs, about 5 eggs
   (at room temperature)
1 cup sugar

When eggs are whipped, sift into them this flour mixture *(measure the flour after sifting, then sift the dry ingredients together)*:
**1 cup plus 1 tablespoon
   sifted cake flour**
1/4 cup sifted pie flour
1 teaspoon salt
**1/4 teaspoon freshly ground
   nutmeg or cardamom seed**
(It is necessary to have this mixture of cake and pie flour to get the right texture in the cake.)

When eggs and flour mixture have been completely combined, just mix in:
2 tablespoons milk
   (at room temperature)
1/2 teaspoon vanilla

Grease 2 cakepans, 1 9–inch and 1 8–inch *(this batter is not enough for 2 9-inch pans, too much for 2 8-inch ones)*. Sift a little flour into the greased pans, shake it around and dump out the excess. This will insure that the cake comes out without sticking.

Fill the tins and bake at 425° for about 12 minutes or until a straw comes out clean. Spread a dish towel and sprinkle granulated sugar on it. Turn the cakes out on this. The sugar will keep them from sticking to the towel.

When they are cool, split each one into 2 layers with a sharp bread knife. Put the bottom half on a plate and spread on a generous amount of custard filling *(recipe on next page)*. Put on top layer of cake and sprinkle it with powdered sugar. As a variation, spread on chocolate icing in place of the powdered sugar.

Makes 2 pies

Custard Filling for Boston Cream Pie

Mix in copper-clad pan so you can boil without burning:
1 1/2 cups whole milk
3/4 cup sugar

Mix with wire whip and add to hot milk; stir vigorously while cooking until it thickens:
1 cup whole milk
3 1/2 tablespoons cornstarch
2 egg yolks
1/8 teaspoon salt
1 teaspoon vanilla
1 tablespoon Myers dark rum
(optional but excellent)

Also optional:
**1 tablespoon grated lemon
 or orange rind**
**1/8 teaspoon cardamom,
 powdered**

When thick, remove from heat and stir in:
1 tablespoon butter

Cool just enough so that filling will not soak into the cake; then spread before a scum forms on the filling. Do not chill this cake; chilling ruins the texture. Serve immediately with plenty of good hot coffee to go with it.

Variation

Prepare:
**3 10-ounce packages frozen,
 sugared red raspberries**
*(defrosted only enough to
 get most of the juice)*

Drain it off and add enough water to make:
1 cup juice

Dissolve:
3 tablespoons cornstarch
1/2 cup water

Add to juice and cook until cornstarch clears. Pour immediately over the raspberries. Stir gently so as not to break up the berries and set aside.

Whip together:
1/2 pint heavy cream
1/2 teaspoon vanilla
3 tablespoons powdered sugar

Pipe the whipped cream around the edge of the cake and pile the fruit in the center. Reserve a dollop of whipped cream to decorate the center. If any whipped cream is left over, it goes with the custard to the cook.

Fresh Fruit Meringue Supreme

Line a very large glass pie plate (*at least 12 inches*) with brown paper, making cuts around the circle of paper so that it will fit down into the plate.

Whip until the whites stand up in peaks:
2/3 cup egg whites
  (*have whites at room temperature; this is important*)

Add gradually, beating in gently just until sugar is dissolved:
1 1/4 cups plus
  1/2 tablespoon sugar

When sugar is dissolved, fold in gently:
3/8 teaspoon vanilla

Spread the meringue in the paper–lined pie plate, taking it up the sides to form a shell to hold the fruit. If your plate isn't large enough to use all of the mixture, make a smaller one, too. It will keep several days quite well.

Bake at 275° for at least 55 minutes. The shell needs to dry out thoroughly. When done, as soon as it is cool enough to handle, turn it over and pull off the paper. Let the meringue cool for at least 1 hour, then brush on the inside a thick coating of:
melted sweet chocolate

This will keep the fruit from soaking the meringue. Put into the refrigerator to chill for at least 1 hour.

Prepare 3 cups of whatever fresh fruit is available, but start with:
1 cup fresh pineapple

With a sharp knife cut off both ends, then stand the pineapple on end and slice down, turn and slice down again, until you have cut off all of the outside blossom remains. Split the fruit in half the long way, then split each half into long fourths. Stand each segment on end and slice off the core part. Lay each piece down and cut it into 1/8-inch pieces. This is the easy way to prepare pineapple.

Mix together:
1/8 teaspoon powdered
  cardamom seed
dash of nutmeg
dash of cinnamon
1 cup honey

Add this mixture to the pineapple and stir well. Peel and slice:
1 large or 2 small bananas

Mix with pineapple immediately; the honey will keep them from turning dark.

Peel and add:
**fresh mandarin orange or
   tangerine segments
other fresh fruit in season,
   sliced or cubed**

Let fruit marinate in the refrigerator for at least 1 hour to blend flavors.

Drain the fruit thoroughly, then fill the meringue with it. Cover with:
whipped cream, sweetened

Garnish with:
**fresh whole strawberries
   or cherries**

Serve thoroughly chilled, cutting the wedges with a sharp knife.

As a variation, put a layer of custard in the meringue before adding the fruit *(see Black Bottom Pie (page 262) for custard recipe)*.

*The desserts
are superb.*

Black Bottom Pie

Years ago when I was traveling in the South, a friend took me to a fine restaurant in Meridian, Mississippi, where one of the specialties of the house was this delicious pie. Of course I asked for the recipe and they readily gave it to me. Several times since, I have found what purported to be black bottom pie, but it certainly wasn't the delicious dessert I had in Meridian. Follow the recipe faithfully and you will add to your fame in the kitchen.

To make the crust, roll to pulverize:
14 gingersnaps

Add and mix together to make an even blend:
5 tablespoons melted butter

Line the bottom of a 9-inch pie pan with this mixture, bake at 450° for 10 minutes and allow to cool.

Put in a double boiler:
2 cups milk, scalding hot

Add and beat in well, one at a time:
4 egg yolks

Combine and stir into milk and egg mixture:
1 1/2 tablespoons cornstarch
1/2 cup sugar

Cook in the double boiler for 20 minutes or until it coats the spoon; then take out 1 cup of the custard and add to it:
1 square of bitter chocolate, shaved fine

Beat this chocolate mixture well as it cools. When cool, spread it evenly on the baked pie shell.

Dissolve:
1 tablespoon gelatin in
2 tablespoons cold water

Add gelatin mixture to custard in the double boiler, mix and allow to cool.

Mix together:
1/2 cup sugar
1/4 teaspoon cream of tartar

Beat until stiff:
4 egg whites

Beat sugar mixture into egg whites only until dissolved, then add and beat in:
2 tablespoons Bourbon whiskey

Gold Layer Cake

Fold this mixture into the remaining custard, mixing in lightly but well, then spread it over the chocolate custard.

Mix together and spread on pie:
1/2 pint heavy cream, whipped
1/3 cup powdered sugar
1/2 teaspoon vanilla

Garnish with long shavings of:
semi–sweet chocolate

Refrigerate before serving.

Put into electric mixing bowl:
9 ounces (*2 1/4 cups sifted*)
 pastry flour
11 ounces (*1 1/2 cups and
 1 tablespoon*) **white sugar**
**4 1/2 teaspoons Calumet
 baking powder**
3 1/2 ounces (*1/2 cup*)
 **shortening such as Spry
 or Crisco**

Beat in half of the following liquid (*scraping down bowl*), for 2 minutes:
**6 ounces refrigerated
 whole milk**
2 ounces very hot water
1 teaspoon vanilla

Add remaining liquid and beat for 1 minute, scraping bowl at least once.

Beat until thick and lemon colored:
7 egg yolks
1 teaspoon salt

Fold into mixture together with:
5 tablespoons cold water

Put into 3 9–inch greased and floured cake pans and bake for 25 minutes at 350°.

Butter cream mint icing or maple icing (*page 266*) goes well with this cake.

Plain Cake, Three Layer

Put in electric mixing bowl:
10 ounces (*2 1/2 cups sifted*)
  pastry flour
12 ounces (*2/3 cup*) **white sugar**
**3 1/2 teaspoons Calumet
  baking powder**
4 ounces (*1/2 cup plus 1 tablespoon*)
  **shortening such as Spry
  or Crisco**
1 teaspoon salt
3 whole eggs
  (*all ingredients at room temperature*)

Add half of the following liquid:
6 ounces milk from refrigerator
2 ounces hot water
1 teaspoon vanilla
(*1/4 teaspoon Mapleine for maple
flavoring if maple cake is being made*)

Beat these ingredients on medium
speed for 2 1/2 minutes, scraping
down bowl at least twice.

Add remaining half of the
liquid and beat for 1 minute.

Turn out batter into 1 9–inch greased
and floured cake pan. Spread batter
to sides of pan leaving it low in
the middle so it will not rise too
high in the center. Bake at 350° for
23 minutes.

To make this a spice cake, omit the
Mapleine and add:
1 1/4 teaspoon cinnamon
1/2 teaspoon nutmeg
1/4 teaspoon cloves, powdered
1/8 teaspoon allspice
**1/4 teaspoon cardamom,
  powdered**

*Wish I dared
ask for a
second dessert.*

Authentic English Pound Cake

Temperature is most important for the success of this cake. Be sure all ingredients are at room temperature, 72°.

Whip until very light and fluffy:
1 pound butter

Add gradually and whip until creamy:
1 pound powdered sugar
   (granulated sugar will not work — it will make the texture too coarse)

Beat in one at a time until well incorporated:
1 pint whole eggs

Add and continue whipping:
1 teaspoon vanilla

Then, while whipping, add slowly the following ingredients which have been well sifted together:
1 pound *(4 cups sifted)*
   pastry flour
1 teaspoon salt
1/2 teaspoon cream of tartar
1/4 teaspoon mace

Put into lightly greased, wax paper–lined bread pans and bake 1 hour at 325°. The top should split slightly. If more time is necessary, leave it in the oven for 5 or 10 minutes longer.

Cream Puffs

Heat together to boiling:
1 cup milk
1/2 cup butter

Add and stir in well:
1 cup bread flour, sifted
1/4 teaspoon salt

Cook until mixture leaves sides of pan *(about 10 minutes)*, then add, 1 at a time, beating after each addition:
4 whole eggs

Spoon batter onto cookie sheet, about 1 tablespoon for each puff, in either rounds or lengths. Bake at 400° for 25 minutes. Reduce heat to 350° and bake 10 minutes longer to dry them out. If they are not thoroughly dry they will not be crisp after taken from oven, and will collapse later, when cool.

Cut and fill with whipped cream or custard *(the custard filling for Boston Cream Pie (page 259) is a good filling for cream puffs)*.

Butterscotch Nut Sticks

Melt in pan on stove:
1/2 cup butter

Add to butter and heat until
it is glossy:
2 cups brown sugar

Remove from heat and cool
slightly, then add:
2 eggs, beaten
1/2 teaspoon vanilla

Mix and then add:
2 cups sifted bread flour
2 teaspoons baking powder
1/2 teaspoon salt

Mix well, then add and mix in:
1 cup chopped nuts,
    any type (walnuts are good)

Spread evenly in greased pan,
10 by 14 inches. Bake at 350° for
25 to 30 minutes. Remove from oven
and cut immediately, before it cools,
into rectangular sticks. Be sure it
is cut all the way through, for
it will harden and become brittle
when cold and will not cut.
Using part black walnuts gives
an excellent flavor.

Butter Cream Mint Icing

Whip in electric mixing bowl:
1/2 cup butter
    (at room temperature)
1/3 cup sour cream
4 tablespoons crème de menthe
    or mint sauce (made by boiling
    2 tablespoons water, 3 tablespoons
    sugar, 1/3 cup mint leaves, and
    3 drops green coloring)

Whip until light, then add powdered
sugar to desired consistency.

Maple Icing with Mapleine

Beat until very light, 5 minutes:
6 ounces (1 1/2 sticks) **butter**
    (at room temperature)

Add and continue beating:
1 1/2 pounds powdered sugar
6 tablespoons coffee cream
1/4 teaspoon Mapleine
1/8 teaspoon vanilla

For additional texture add and
beat for 1 minute:
1/2 cup chopped walnuts

Apple Pie

The great "Mom and Apple Pie" era seems to have gone out of our national consciousness. Here is a recipe that should help to revive it. The apples should be the tart variety, like Pippins or Granny Smith.

For 1 pie the following amounts are suggested:

Mix together and then stir into 2 quarts of cut apples:
3/4 cup sugar
1/2 teaspoon cinnamon
1/4 teaspoon nutmeg

Thicken with:
1 tablespoon starch, dissolved in a little water

Mix the spice and sugar mixture with the apples. Let stand for about 2 hours, mixing frequently so all slices will be coated with the sugar mixture. Drain the juice from the apples and reserve it.

Fill the pie crust which has been prepared *(page 268)*, heaping the apples up to make a very full pie. *(This pie will not boil over in the oven because the juice has been extracted by the sugar.)* Lay on the top crust, crimping the edges. **Do not punch a hole in the top crust as it will let the steam out, which cooks the apples.**

Bake at about 400° until crust is nicely brown. Remove the pie and with a funnel inserted in the top crust pour in the juice which has been prepared in the following way.

Heat the juice in kettle, and thicken it with a little starch dissolved in a little water. Taste it and if necessary, the apples not being tart enough, add a very small amount of lemon juice. Some cooks like to enhance the flavor with a small amount of pineapple juice.

The apples will absorb the juice like little sponges. The crust will have been baked crisp and dry. Mom will have been reinstated in her former place of honor in the forum of things gone past.

Fig & Blueberry Pie

Melt and spread evenly on the bottom of a pie pastry shell:
1 ounce semi–sweet chocolate

Spread thin layer of blueberry sauce in bottom of shell. On top of this place sliced figs. Follow with another layer of blueberry sauce and then sliced figs. Top with about 1/4–inch custard, then finish with Cassias cream. Decorate with fresh sliced figs and blueberries.

Crust for Top & Bottom of a 9-inch Pie Plate

In a mixer combine:
2 1/2 cups white bread flour
1 teaspoon salt

With 2 knives or pastry blender, cut flour to form a coarse mix the size of marbles. Add:
3/4 cup vegetable shortening
1/4 cup butter

Shape mixture into flat pieces and do not overmix. Make a hole in the center of the mix and pour in 1/2 cup ice water. Quickly mix together with a spoon only enough to enable you to handle the dough. Turn dough out onto a lightly floured board and divide in half. Roll out into circles 1/8–inch thick or less.

Custard

In a saucepan cook until thick, stirring constantly:
3/4 cup light cream
1/2 cup heavy cream
3/8 cup sugar
2 egg yolks
4 tablespoon cornstarch
1 teaspoon vanilla
1 teaspoon butter

Blueberry Sauce

In a saucepan cook until thick, stirring constantly:
1 basket fresh blueberries
1/4 cup Cassias syrup
1/2 cup sugar
2 tablespoons cornstarch

Cassias Cream

Whip in mixing bowl until thick:
1 cup heavy cream
2 tablespoons Cassias syrup

Chambord Crème

Whip until stiff but not dry:
1 pint whipping cream

Add and fold in gently:
2 tablespoons powdered sugar
1 1/2 teaspoons stabilizer

Then add and fold in:
4 ounces Chambord liqueur

Spoon the above crème over fresh red raspberries.

Amaretto Chocolate Supreme

Put into blender:
5 egg yolks

In fairly large pan, melt until smooth:
8 ounces semi–sweet chocolate pieces
1 teaspoon almond extract
1 tablespoon amaretto
1 teaspoon instant coffee
pinch of salt

Bring just to boil, then pour into blender and whirl for 10 seconds:
1 cup whipping cream

Add cream to chocolate mixture and beat until smooth. Pour into 4–ounce champagne glasses and refrigerate for at least 4 hours.

To serve, top with whipped cream that has been flavored with amaretto. Sprinkle on crushed, slivered or sliced almonds. This dessert can be frozen. Also good served with Pistachio Cream Sauce (*page 42*).

Raspberry Glaze
for Cake

Thaw a 5–pound bag of raspberries reserving the juice, which should be 2 1/2 cups.

Mix together, cook until thick:
2 1/2 cups juice
5 tablespoons starch

Add and stir in and cook until smooth:
3 pounds white sugar
pinch salt
3 tablespoons tapioca flour

Cool before spreading on top of sponge cake.

Pineapple Guava Sorbet

This sorbet is made with the meat of the guava so it has a bit of a grainy texture, but a wonderful piney flavor. Peel and purée in blender enough guavas to make 4 cups. This should be done just before freezing, or the purée will oxidize and turn dark.

Bring to a boil:
1 cup water
1 cup sugar

Then cool completely and add:
4 cups guava purée
2 tablespoons lemon juice

Put in ice cream freezer and freeze.

Dessert Crêpes

Combine in blender:

2 eggs
2 egg yolks
1/2 cup water
1/2 cup milk
2 teaspoons dark sesame oil
1 teaspoon peanut oil
1/2 cup fruit juice
    (*orange preferably*)
1/4 cup sugar
1/8 teaspoon salt
1 cup flour

To make the crêpes:

Pour 2 ounces batter into a non-stick pan. Turn pan to spread batter evenly over bottom of pan. Cook about 40 to 60 seconds until brown on one side. Turn crêpe and cook for about 10 seconds more.

The first couple of crêpes may not work out, so do a few more until pan is properly seasoned. To prevent sticking, the pan may be wiped with a little peanut oil between crêpes.

For use on fruit crêpes:

Lemon Cream Sauce

Melt:
8 ounces butter

Add, heat and stir until sugar dissolves:
1 1/2 cups sugar
1 1/2 cups lemon juice
zest from 1 lemon

Beat together and add to above:
3 whole eggs
3 egg yolks

Simmer the above until thick, then add:
1 cup heavy cream (*or thereabout, to desired consistency*)

Cranberry Bourbon Sorbet

In a stainless steel saucepan
combine:
2 1/4 cups water
1 1/2 cups sugar

Bring the mixture to a boil over
moderate heat, stirring until sugar is
dissolved, then add:
1 pound cranberries

Simmer covered, 5 to 7 minutes or
until berries have popped and are
soft. Cool for 10 minutes. Blend
and strain through fine sieve into a
bowl, pressing hard on the solids.

Now add:
3 tablespoons Bourbon

Freeze in ice cream freezer.

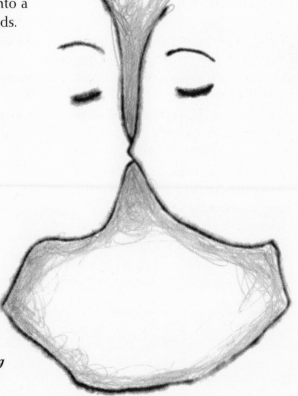

*Let's think
about something
besides food.*